W9-BUB-705

Mother's Wisdom

A BOOK OF THOUGHTS
AND ENCOURAGEMENTS

R. D. Ramsey

CB

CONTEMPORARY
BOOKS

A TRIBUNE NEW MEDIA COMPANY

Library of Congress Cataloging-in-Publication Data

Ramsey, Robert D.
    Mother's wisdom : a book of thoughts and
encouragements / Robert D. Ramsey.
        p.   cm.
    ISBN 0-8092-3433-5
    1. Mothers—Quotations, maxims, etc.   2. Children—
Quotations, maxims, etc.   3. Conduct of life—
Quotations, maxims, etc.   I. Title.
PN6084.M6R36   1995
306.874'3—dc20   95-2993
                                                  CIP

Copyright © 1995 by Robert D. Ramsey
All rights reserved
Published by Contemporary Books, Inc.
Two Prudential Plaza, Chicago, Illinois 60601-6790
Manufactured in the United States of America
International Standard Book Number: 0-8092-3433-5
10   9   8   7   6   5   4   3   2   1

This book is dedicated to Eva Diehl Ramsey and Olive Layman Lundry—two loving mothers who succeeded as single parents long before it was fashionable.

FOREWORD

"Mother is the name for God in the lips and hearts of children."

William Makepeace Thackeray

*M*otherhood is the most demanding, most wonderful work in the world. Mothers have to be dynamite every day. They work long hours. They're on call twenty-four hours a day. Their weekends are never free. They get few vacations. They can't resign, and they never retire. The pay is indefinite, but it's all worth it, because their product is the future.

Mother's Wisdom can help in building tomorrow by providing a daily boost of inspiration and motivation for all mothers.

Its positive messages and affirmations on the joys, pain, and pathos of motherhood are surefire antidotes for burnout and boredom in society's toughest role.

Each commonsense thought is designed for single and married mothers from all kinds of nuclear, blended, and extended families. Every upbeat reflection will help you become the best mother (and the best person) you can be, without shame or guilt.

These encouraging thoughts can provide just the insight, lift, or laugh you need to be the mother your children deserve. They offer quick reading with long-lasting results. Why not start enjoying them now?

Mother's Wisdom

Babe Ruth struck out 1,333 times.

Everyone needs to start over or try again sometimes. As the great Babe Ruth proved, yesterday's strikeout doesn't mean that today can't be a hit.

All children—and adults—should be able to fail without feeling like failures. Resiliency means learning from our misses and coming back from our losses.

I will give my kids—and myself—lots of fresh starts and second chances. That's how we grow strong. It worked for Babe Ruth!

1

"I've learned that love will break your heart, but it's worth it."

Twenty-six-year-old mother,
Live & Learn & Pass It On

emember these rules, advise mothers everywhere, to survive motherhood with joy:
1. Expect your children to hurt you deeply—more than once.
2. Expect to get over it.

**I will remind myself that the love
will outlast the pain.**

"Quarrels are the weapons of the weak."
Laurie Baker

Quarreling is learned behavior—children raised in a house of quarrels become quarrelers themselves.

Arguing shouldn't become a family tradition. We can do better.

**I will demonstrate positive ways to resolve
conflicts with others so my children
become strong adults.**

3

"A mother understands what a child does not say."
Jewish proverb

*S*ometimes what is left unsaid between a mother and child is more important than what is said. Some feelings are too big to be put into little words. "Pay attention" is not always easy advice to follow, but kids count on their mothers to hear the unspoken. And mothers who learn to read unspoken cues and clues say it only brings them closer to their children.

I will watch for signs of what my children are feeling. I won't wait for their words to catch up with their emotions.

4

"Imagination is more important than knowledge."
Albert Einstein

*E*very child has a vivid imagination. Unfortunately, a lot of it gets lost somewhere along the way to adulthood. Yet once we've arrived at adulthood, most of us would agree that there ought to be more to life than reality.

Imagination can make both your children and their lives more interesting. Cultivate it.

I will celebrate my child's imagination. It's the last thing I want to shut down.

"Solitude is not a luxury. It is a right and a necessity."

Anne Wilson Schaef

*B*eing a mother means always doing things in a crowd. Children come at you from all directions. Demands are unceasing. It's an on-call, twenty-four-hour-a-day job. Nevertheless, smart mothers know they must take care of themselves first, or they won't be able to care for others later on.

You need some quiet time for yourself each day. Small doses of silence and solitude do more for a mother's sanity than tranquilizers can ever do.

I will find time to be alone. I owe it to myself and to my family.

"How old would you be if you didn't know how old you was?"

Satchel Paige

*T*hose who haven't tried it often think motherhood causes premature aging. You're in the lucky position to know that motherhood actually keeps you young.

The childhood years go by so fast that there's no time to think about age.

I know I must be young. I'm a mother.

"Children are the keys to paradise."
                                        Richard Henry Stoddard

*E*verybody knows that children are a burden and a responsibility. They're distractions, interruptions, and inconveniences. They cost lots of money and monopolize your time. They get into trouble and drag you into it with them. They worry you constantly. Everybody knows this about kids.

Mothers know something more. Children make life worthwhile. They reward you a hundredfold without even trying. It doesn't get any better than having kids. Mothers know this; they just aren't telling. (Who would believe them?)

**I will keep the secret all mothers know—
children are worth it!**

"All great changes are irksome to the human mind."
John Adams

*C*hange is a necessary nuisance. It's what motherhood is all about. From diapers to attitudes to habits, mothers are change agents all their lives. According to a joke often repeated among mothers, as soon as you've adjusted to a difficult developmental stage, your child moves on to the next one.

If nothing ever changed or needed changing, mothers would be out of work. Those mothers who seem to have it all adopt this principle: master change and make it happen.

**I will accept—and welcome—change
as a way of life.**

9

"Learn to pause . . . or nothing worthwhile will catch up with you."

Doug Kling

$\mathcal{S}$ometimes stopping is better than going. Only if you stop frequently to listen to your children will you really see them as they are. They will never look the same again.

Pauses can be the best part of the day. Use them often to keep in touch with your world.

**I will stop long enough to appreciate
what's really going on
with myself and with my children.**

"Children need love, especially when they do not deserve it."

Harold S. Hulbert

Anybody can love a child when things are good. What makes mothers special is that they love their children even when things are rotten.

A mother's love is not dependent on anything. But on some days children make it a challenge to show them that you'll love them no matter what. Those are, unfortunately, the days when they need to know it the most.

———————   ———————

**I will remember that children need love most
when they are most unlovable,
and I will show my children that my love
will never fail them.**

11

"Sometimes dreams are wiser than waking."
William Least Heat-Moon

A child's dreams are fragile, and the world is full of people who delight in stomping on them. With their mothers, however, children's dreams are safe.

Don't expect your child to share dreams unless you're willing to respect and protect them. Never pooh-pooh them. If the two of you believe, your child's dreams just might come true.

I will support my child's dreams and never laugh at them. They will be safe with me.

"Few things help an individual more than to place responsibility upon him and to let him know that you trust him."

Booker T. Washington

Responsibility is a growth hormone for self-confidence. Children thrive on responsibility. They see it as a vote of confidence from adults.

The only way young people can learn to be responsible is to have responsibility. This is one thing all parents can give to their children.

I will remember that my child can and will live up to great expectations.

*"Broken hearts heal slowly, but a speedy application
of chocolate can often help stop the initial bleeding."*
Ashleigh Brilliant

*C*hildren are easily hurt—on the inside and the outside.
It usually doesn't last long. Sometimes a little treat
helps.

Dr. Mom always keeps a little candy around for medicinal
purposes.

**I will prescribe candy when appropriate.
(Whatever works!)**

"The higher you climb up the company ladder, the later you get home from work."

Bruce Lansky

As a working mother, you don't take your children to work every day; so don't bring your work home to your children every night.

Both kids and careers need their own time and place. Give each its due.

I won't step on my children while climbing the ladder of success.

"All children wear the sign 'I want to be important NOW.' "

Dan Pursuit

Children live in a world of immediacy. They don't understand the concept of delayed gratification.

You can't put children's needs on hold. "I'll get back to you later" doesn't work with kids. They don't know how to wait until it's convenient to get the attention they need.

Hug your child now. Listen to your child now. Praise your child now. To children, *now* is the only time there is.

**I won't keep my children waiting
for my love.**

16

"Childhood is frequently a solemn business for those inside it."

George Will

The worries of children just don't seem very big to most grown-ups, but childish things aren't childish to children. Their problems are as significant to them as ours are to us.

Thoughtful mothers never forget what it was like to be a child. Remember: if your child thinks something is important, it's important.

I will look at my children's problems from their level. It doesn't help to look down on them.

"And all my toys beside me lay. . . ."
                                        Robert Louis Stevenson

Sometimes a toy can be a kid's best friend. Toys don't give orders, don't interrupt, and stay where you put them. That's what friends are for.

Avoid making fun of your children's attachments to their favorite toys, and maybe they won't make fun of yours. Both children and adults need all the comforting they can get.

I will respect my child's favorite toy.

"Parenthood is one of the last frontiers."

Phil Batchelor

All mothers and fathers chart unknown territory in raising each new child. Every life has its own map.

Don't be afraid to try something different with your child. You're a pathfinder. No one else has ever raised your child before.

Making history is part of being a mother.

**I will be a pioneer,
and I will enjoy the journey.**

19

*"Instant availability without continuous presence is
probably the best role a mother can play."*

Lotte Bailyn

There's a difference between mothering and smothering.
All children want parents to be there for them without
being around all the time.

Good parents know how to be out of sight without being
out of touch.

**I will be sure my children know I am always
just a phone call away.**

"Every child is different."

Anon.

At birth, all mothers know their child is special. From that moment on, however, the world tries to make a child fit a preconceived mold. Children are supposed to dress like other kids, eat what other kids eat, and act like other children their age. The kids feel this pressure, and so do their mothers.

Everyone else will try to force your child to conform. You're in a unique position to celebrate each child's differences.

**I will champion my child's uniqueness
in the world.**

"Without music life would be a mistake."
                                    Friedrich Nietzsche

*L*ife goes better with music, and children are natural
    musicians.

Music is a voice that speaks across classes and nationalities.
It comforts, motivates, inspires, and entertains people of all
ages.

Music can be either a centerpiece or a backdrop for living.
Don't let your child grow up without it.

I will enjoy music with my child every day.

"Touch is not a pleasant stimulus but a biological necessity."

Phyllis Davis

Touch is a powerful nutrient to the psyche. We all need it. Children, particularly, need the support and intimacy provided by physical contact with loved ones.

Follow your instincts to touch and hug your children. Don't worry about whether the time is right or the circumstances appropriate. Physical reinforcement of your love and support is a very real source of strength.

———————— ————————

**I won't just tell my children I love them;
I will show them through
affectionate touch.**

"To have it all, don't do it all."

Anne Weisberg

Working moms have become the norm. Balancing work and family requires adjustments on the home front and in the workplace. Trying to be "Supermom" is unfair—to everyone around you, but especially to yourself. Everyone needs to do his or her part.

Give yourself a break. Others can help. Don't try to be perfect at everything. You'll only set yourself up for failure at home and on the job.

I'll honor my commitments by doing the best I can. I won't try to do more.

"Nobody ever went to college with a pacifier."

Anon.

$\mathcal{L}$ots of infants suck their thumbs or a pacifier. It's a sign they're trying to comfort themselves rather than relying on others for comfort.

What comforts the child, however, can disturb the mother. Some families get caught in a power struggle over thumb sucking. It's not worth it.

It's better to relax and help the child find a substitute source of comfort. The practice will run its course. Thumb sucking isn't a lifelong problem.

I'll do what I can to make my child feel secure and not worry about habits that will eventually go away anyway.

"Nothing is particularly hard if you break it down into small jobs."

Henry Ford

Sometimes life seems overwhelming to children. It's too big for them to get their arms around.

Show your child how to break big jobs into manageable tasks. It's a skill that will serve them all their lives.

Puzzles don't come together all at once. We put them together a piece at a time.

I'll show my child that the only way to get anywhere is one step at a time.

"Happiness is a choice."

Barry Kaufman

*W*hat life does to us is largely a by-product of how we look at it. We're in charge of our attitude, and our attitude controls our feelings.

When you choose to be happy, you show your child that hope is always an option.

I will give my child the gift of happiness by being happy myself.

"A 'good mother' always notices more good than bad in their children."

Daniel Amen

Criticism can be constructive, but praise is better. One loud cheer for picked-up toys will get you a neat room faster than days of scolding.

Mothers learn to overlook lots of warts. They gladly take the job as their child's biggest fan.

I'll catch my children being good, and I'll tell them about it.

"Technology is a way of life."

Anon.

*M*odern mothers wisely tap modern technology to stay close to children who are far away. Today's "information highway" can lead over the river and through the woods to Grandma's house or to wherever children are scattered.

E-mail now connects millions of people. Why not use this technology to network among family members? It's quicker than the postal service, and no one has to be there to receive the call.

I will learn how to log on with my children to help hold the family together.

"Nothing great was ever achieved without enthusiasm."

Ralph Waldo Emerson

*E*nthusiasm shows. If you're excited about being a mother, your son or daughter will be more excited about being your child.

I'll let my children see how much I like being their mother.

"Women keep their eye on the ball."

Wilma Mankiller

*B*eing a mother requires focus. There are lots of distractions when kids are around. All kinds of things are always happening at once. Successful mothers learn to concentrate on major issues.

Don't dissipate energy on trifles. Pay attention to the basics, and the details will take care of themselves. Remember that you're only one person and you can't take care of everything.

**I'll concentrate most on what's most
important and take care of the big things first.**

"Truth does not blush."

                                                        Tertullian

*M*any people aren't bothered by telling little white lies. They feel it's easier than dealing with awkward truths. It doesn't work with children, however.

Kids are automatically honest. They don't deal in guile, and they don't understand when adults lie to them. It makes them feel used and betrayed.

You never have to be embarrassed to tell your children the truth.

I'll tell my children the truth even when it would be easier to lie a little.

"Every child is an artist. The problem is how to remain an artist once he grows up."

Pablo Picasso

Children are creative creatures. They love to dabble in clay and revel in the joy of colors. Drawing and painting are magical pastimes for little children.

Kids are expressive artists until adults start telling them there are rules or begin trying to influence how their artwork should look. That's when many children lose interest.

Encourage your children to explore art their way and have fun with it. Save the rules for later.

I won't worry if my children color outside the lines.

"The best you can get is an even break."
                              Franklin Pierce Adams

We do our children a disservice when we show favoritism or seek preferential treatment for them. It can lead to a false sense of security or superiority.

Anything gained through unearned advantage is neither appreciated nor valued. The sweetest rewards are those achieved through effort. Children grow strong by getting things on their own, not by having things given to them.

**I'll help my children succeed by letting them
try, fail, and try again on their own.**

"We are, perhaps, uniquely among the earth's creatures, the worrying animal."

Lewis Thomas

Mothers worry a lot. It usually doesn't help, and they lose a lot of sleep in the process.

Worrying is inventing your own worst nightmares while you're still awake. It's not productive the way planning and problem solving are.

Worse, it's contagious. Children become anxious when their mothers worry too much.

I'll do what I can and then let go so my children and I can enjoy the peace of mind we've earned.

"No one ever kept a secret better than a child."
Victor Hugo

$\mathcal{S}$haring a secret with a child builds a special bond. It makes the child feel important and more grown up. For the moment the two of you are equals.

Children love secrets. Even more, they love being entrusted with them.

---— ———

**I will show my trust by sharing
a secret with my child.**

"There ain't no sense gettin' riled up."

Bret Harte

*A*nger isn't a pretty emotion. It's hurtful and harmful. No problem has ever been solved by anger.

Anger can make children out of grown-ups. Little children get angry and throw tantrums because they're children. Successful mothers don't get angry; they hold their temper because they're adults.

Kids will test you and tire you, but they don't have to anger you.

I will not let my children make me angry.

*"Every generation revolts against its fathers and
makes friends with its grandfathers."*

Lewis Mumford

Children who have grandparents in their lives are doubly
blessed.

You can't have too many helping hands, listening ears, or
loving hearts around when you're a child. That's what grandparents are for. They give unconditional love just as parents do,
but they don't care if they spoil the child in the process.

Grandparents are too good a thing for kids to miss out on.

**I'll look for extra opportunities to include
grandparents in my child's life.**

"God is a friend of silence."

Mother Teresa

S ome mothers are afraid of quiet. They don't know how to be with their children without talking to them. The truth is that love doesn't require conversation. Sometimes silence is the best sound of all. It can be spiritual and healing. Teach your child to enjoy quietude and to listen to the silence together sometimes.

I'll be quiet with my child for a little while.

"Talk low, talk slow, and don't say too much."
John Wayne

*K*ids should learn that the loudest mouth isn't always listened to most. Nobody likes people who talk too much or too loudly or always say inappropriate things.

Smart mouths and loud mouths get no respect. Speech is a gift. It's not intended to be used as a weapon.

**I'll show my children how to stop
and think before speaking.**

"Few things are harder to put up with than the annoyance of a good example."

Mark Twain

There's such a thing as being too much of a role model. Perfection is a turnoff. No one wants to have to live up to a mother who's bigger than life. Most kids would rather have a mother who's human.

Don't live a lie. Be yourself. It's better than being perfect.

**I won't be afraid to admit my mistakes
and own my weaknesses.**

"Manners are greater than laws."

Ralph Waldo Emerson

In many ways our society has lost its manners. Civility is not in style. Meanness has replaced manners, and the world is a more unpleasant place to live in because of it.

The only way to return to a society where people are polite and show respect for one another is to rebuild it one family at a time. Why not start with yours?

Teach your child manners. It's not old-fashioned. It's called civilization.

**I will teach my children that manners
are not silly rules but a way of showing
kindness to everyone.**

"It is impossible to overemphasize the immense need human beings have to be really listened to, to be taken seriously, to be understood."

Paul Tournier

It's tempting to try to get close to your children by giving them the trappings of life. If you do, you're giving all the wrong things.

The truth is that the best gift for any child is a parent's undivided attention. To be a great parent, just take the time to really get to know your child.

I will listen to my children as closely as I listen to adults.

"Our life is frittered away by detail . . . Simplify, simplify."

Henry David Thoreau

For a child, life is as simple as adults make it. Some mothers make their child's life overly complicated by cramming in too many activities and choices. Children need to grow without being overwhelmed.

Give your children only as much life as they can handle at one time.

I will be careful not to burden my children with more activities than they can handle and enjoy.

"We won't have a society if we destroy the environment."

Margaret Mead

*C*hildren are our best environmentalists. They love nature and haven't acquired bad habits of excessive consumption. Where recycling can be a chore for adults, it's a game for kids.

If we can teach young children to preserve the environment, they may teach all of us in the long run. It would take only one generation of ecology-conscious citizens to make peace with the environment.

We will plan ways that all members of our family can help save the environment.

"Traditions are the crossroads between the old and the new."

Maryann and Carl Elkins

*R*ituals provide anchors in our lives. Every family needs traditions that reflect common values and beliefs. They let our children know what we stand for and care about. They are windows to our heritage.

Traditions remind us all of things that don't change. They are yesterday's memories acted out over and over to keep them fresh. They add stability, meaning, comfort, and security to our hurried existence. This is important to children and adults alike.

**I will give my child a role in our unique
family traditions.**

*"Cleaning your house while your kids are still
growing is like shoveling the walk before it stops
snowing."*

Phyllis Diller

Tidiness and children don't always get along together.
Neatness requires order and organization. Growing
children need spontaneity and a little chaos.

You can have a well-kept home anytime. Your children
will be small only once. The priorities are obvious. Even a
messy room can be beautiful in a mother's eyes.

**I won't worry about an unkempt house as
long as my child's life is in order.**

"Simply having children does not make mothers."
John A. Shedd

$\mathcal{M}$ost women can have babies, but motherhood is an earned state. You have to work at it. Being a good mother is more than biology. It requires sacrifice, hard work, lots of time, and a willingness to keep learning every day and never give up.

It takes nine months to have a baby. It takes a lifetime to become a mother.

I will pay the price of being a good mother by giving my time, my love, and my best every waking moment.

"There is more to life than increasing its speed."
Mahatma Gandhi

*E*verybody complains about the pace of life, yet we're the ones who set the speed. If we don't like the rat race, we don't have to run.

Neither should our children. It's hard not to hurry them when they take fifteen minutes to tie one shoe, but rushing may rob them of much of the joy of their accomplishment. Slow down when you can so both of you can revel in their work. The precious moments of childhood are all too fleeting as it is.

**I will show my child that getting there
is half the fun.**

"A mother is not a person to lean on but a person to make leaning unnecessary."

Dorothy Canfield Fisher

*M*others are naturally protective and supportive, but it's not their responsibility to carry children all through life. Motherhood is about teaching independence.

The best mothers work themselves out of a large part of their job. Success is being needed less and less as your child grows.

Help your child become competent and you'll be needed less but wanted more. Your children will never outgrow you.

**I won't be afraid to let my children do more
and more things on their own.
(I may even push them a little bit.)**

"Parents should be enjoying life."

Paul W. Robinson

arenting is serious business and a heavy responsibility, but none of us are going to do it perfectly, so we might as well lighten up.

Being a mother or father can be fun if we let it. It just takes seeing the silliness in much of what we do and not taking ourselves too seriously. Kids do funny things. Grown-ups do even more. Be willing to see the humor in every situation. Laughter is contagious.

I won't be a grim mother.
I don't want to raise a grim child.

"Man is a tool-using animal."

Thomas Carlyle

*C*hildren are natural builders. They love to see things come together. There is no greater pride than a child's feeling of accomplishment upon constructing something.

Parents should teach kids how to use tools to fix things and to build things. It provides some lifelong skill and a boost to a child's self-confidence at the same time.

I will get my children some simple tools of their own and show them how to use them.

"The trouble with experts is that they tend to think in grooves."

Elaine Morgan

*E*verybody is an expert on child rearing. As a mother, you will never have a shortage of advice.

The truth is that there are no all-knowing experts; there is no one right way to raise a child. All the world's self-appointed authorities don't know your child and your situation as well as you do. Trust your instincts.

I will remember that in one area I have more education than anyone else: knowing my child.

"Let there be spaces in your togetherness."

Kahlil Gibran

*F*amily closeness doesn't negate the need for privacy. As much as children thrive on parental presence and support, they also need opportunities for some time alone and the company of their own thoughts.

There's such a thing as too much togetherness. You don't always have to be physically present to be there for your kids. Good mothers know when to back off.

I will not violate my child's right to privacy.

"Parents are allowed 20,000 mistakes before they have to apply for a refill."

Lawrence Kuiner

$\mathcal{S}$ ometimes we become paralyzed by the paranoia of parenthood. We are immobilized by fear of making a mistake, afraid that any wrong decision may crush our child's psyche forever. We anguish too much.

All mothers and fathers make mistakes—lots of them. Kids survive anyway. They're a lot tougher than we think they are.

Don't be afraid to make mistakes. Your batting average will be as good as anyone else's.

I will trust myself and my child to learn from my mistakes.

"Minds, like bodies, will often fall into a pimpled,
ill-conditioned state from mere excess of comfort."
Charles Dickens

*C*omfort is not a condition of growth. Successful mothers stir things up once in a while.

Don't let your kids get into a rut. Keep prodding them to try new activities, make new friends, and keep learning new things all the time. There's enough time for comfort in old age.

**I will generate some positive discomfort
in my kids. We'll try some new ways
of doing things.**

"I had nothing to offer anybody except my own confusion."

Jack Kerouac

*D*are to be confused. It's a natural state of motherhood. Raising children is a confusing process. Be wary of those mothers who act certain of what they're doing.

Never apologize for your confusion. Enjoy it. Sometimes we have to be confused before we can see clearly later on.

❧

I will share my confusion. Part of motherhood is muddling through.

"Half the modern drugs could well be thrown out the window, except that the birds might eat them."

Martin H. Fischer

*S*ome mothers think raising kids is a chemistry experiment. They constantly give their children vitamins, supplements, and medication for all of life's aches and pains, whether real or imagined.

Don't get in the habit of giving your child lots of drugs and medications. Good health doesn't come from a medicine chest. Children grow strong through healthy living. Nature is the best pharmacy.

I will avoid giving my children any drugs, pills, or medications that they don't absolutely have to take.

" 'Curiouser and curiouser,' cried Alice."

Lewis Carroll

Curiosity may have killed the cat, but it's children's lifeblood. Encourage your children to be curious. It drives their learning.

Pity the poor child who doesn't have more questions than answers.

I will welcome questions and refrain from penalizing curiosity.

"Work is much more fun than fun."

The Observer

*H*elp your children make a game out of doing their household chores. Associating work with pleasure is a lifelong survival skill. People who can find fun in their work are happier and more productive. It all begins by having fun with the little things children have to do around the house.

**I will show my children that work and play
aren't that far apart.**

"Sometimes give your service for nothing."

Hippocrates

It's OK to pay your kids for some of the things they do. It's not OK to pay them for everything they do. Children need to learn the joy of contributing with no strings attached.

The world would be a much poorer, sadder place if we had to pay for everything people do for us.

I will use my own volunteer work to teach my children the value of doing something for others.

"For everything there is a season."

Ecclesiastes 3:1

here's a reason for seasons. They give rhythm to our lives. The cycle of seasons teaches us that, while things change, they remain the same. Each season is new all over again. You can count on seasons.

Celebrate each new season with your child. From summer picnics to winter sledding, there are special things you can do with your children each season of the year.

**I will note the beginning of a new season
with my child and use it as an excuse for all
of us to get a fresh start.**

"Any idiot can face a crisis—it's the day-to-day living that wears you out."

Anton Chekhov

The true test of a good mother is how she functions when the adrenaline stops flowing. Lots of people can rise to the occasion in an emergency but don't wear well over the long run of routine life. It takes tenacity to handle the nitty-gritty of raising children.

Mothers don't have to be heroes. They just have to be able to be up when they feel down and to hang in there all day every day.

**I will find one small thing worth celebrating
in every routine day.**

"You can't make an omelet without breaking eggs."
Proverb

*S*ome mothers are afraid to try anything new for fear of making a mess or disturbing other people or things. Change is messy. Don't worry about it.

It's better to break eggs and make an omelet than to walk on eggs and make nothing.

––––––––––– ❦ –––––––––––

I will be willing to tolerate some routine upheaval in order to create something new and worthwhile.

"Nothing succeeds like success."
                                    Alexandre Dumas père

*S*uccess is a little like eating popcorn. You don't know how good it is until the first taste. After that you want more, and each bite goes down easier.

Some people don't know they can succeed until they do. Then they acquire an "I can" attitude. Once people experience success, they know what it feels like and what it takes to get it. Future successes come more easily.

Set your children up for success. They'll take it from there.

**Every day we will do some things I know my
children can succeed at.**

"Plan your work for today and every day, then work your plan."

Norman Vincent Peale

*L*ife without a plan is chaos. Some people let things happen to them. Others make things happen according to plan. The latter are called *leaders*.

Teach your children to have a plan and how to plan. It's the only way they can control their lives and make things come out the way they want.

Some people plan without doing. Some do without planning. Winners both plan and do.

**I will show my children how
I plan for the day.**

"I was shipwrecked before I got aboard."
Lucius Annaeus Seneca the Younger

S ome people are defeated before they start just because they think they are. They're losers in their own minds. They never make it because they never really try.

Failure can be self-fulfilling, but so can success.

Don't let your children write themselves off without a try. Teach them to take a shot. Mothers have to give pep talks sometimes.

**I will teach my children to try new things
without fear of failure.**

"The only good budget is a balanced budget."
                                            Adam Smith

When your budget is out of control, your whole life is out of control. You'll do your children a major favor if you teach them how to handle and budget money at an early age.

Fortunately, children are natural collectors and hoarders. This can apply to money as well as to dolls or baseball cards. Learning to manage money can be like a game to kids.

If you teach your children to budget while they're young, they'll be ahead all their lives.

**I will help my children set up a simple
budget for their money.**

"Work is love made visible."

Kahlil Gibran

*S*ome children don't understand when their mother has to work instead of staying and playing with them. This can create a major guilt trip for Mom.

The truth is that working to make life better for your children is the best kind of love. Teach them that working is required to provide the necessities and comforts you want to give them because you love them.

I will work as much as I have to and play with my kids as much as I can and not feel guilty about it. I am only one person.

"The greatest terror a child can have is that he is not loved and rejection is the hell he fears."

John Steinbeck

Wise mothers want discipline to be an act of love, not rejection. When you have to impose consequences, your children should never be allowed to feel that your love is contingent on good behavior.

I will let my children know I love them even when I don't like what they do.

"Unexpressed feelings never die; they just get buried and come forth later in uglier form."

Linda and Richard Eyre

Repressed feelings are time bombs. Sometimes children don't tell us how they feel because we act as if we already know. Instead of saying "I know how that must have made you feel," why not ask, "How did that make you feel?" You might be surprised by the answer.

The best way to help children let out their feelings, however, is to share some of your own. Self-disclosure is a powerful bonding agent.

**I will share some of my feelings with
my children and encourage them to
share some of theirs.**

"Our children will be as courteous and respectful to others as we are to them."

Phil Batchelor

Courtesy and respect are among those things that you have to give away to receive. It works with kids as well as with adults. (Respect isn't something you reserve for grown-ups.)

With children, you pretty much reap what you sow. They mirror adult behavior. If you are polite and respectful to children, they'll be courteous and respectful to you.

I will show my children the respect I want them to show to me and others.

"A bookstore is one of the only pieces of physical evidence we have that people are still thinking."
Jerry Seinfeld

Bookstores are wondrous places for children. In a bookstore a child can browse, meet real live authors, and listen to stories. Some stores even cater to kids by offering a full range of book events for children of all ages.

Bookstores don't replace libraries, but all kids love owning some special favorite books. Introduce your child to the joy of bookstore hopping.

I will take my child on bookstore adventures—even when all we intend to do is browse.

"Children have more need of models than of critics."
Joseph Soubert

*M*ost adults are better at criticizing kids than at showing them how to live. All grown-ups think they know what's wrong with today's younger generation and are willing to share their wisdom. It's like Monday-morning quarterbacking every day of the week.

Children don't need more critics sitting on the sideline. They need people willing to get into the arena and demonstrate responsible living.

Talk is cheap. Adults, especially parents, have to walk the walk to make a difference with kids.

I will live my advice.

"A promise made is a debt unpaid."
                              Robert William Service

*K*ids take promises seriously. Adults should too. Nothing hurts more than the broken promise of a loved one.

Like faith, once broken, a promise is a hard thing to put back together again.

Keep your word if you would keep your child's trust.

--- ⇛ ---

I will honor any promise I make to my child.

75

"You can learn from monks and hermits without becoming one."

Linus Mundy

Even mothers need to be alone sometimes. Privacy isn't just for teenagers.

The time you spend alone creates a better you to spend time with your children and others later on.

Don't be afraid to hibernate now and then.

_____ _____

**I will plan to take a day off
by myself for myself.**

"I know I must write. If I don't write, I'll die."
James T. Farrell

There's a writer in every child. When adults avoid stifling their creativity with too many rules, kids write their hearts out.

Writing is a way for children (and adults) to have fun with words, polish language skills, organize thoughts, express feelings, and give substance to unspoken dreams.

Release the author in your children. Encourage their writing without fussing too much over spelling and grammar errors. That can come later.

---   ---

**I will urge my children to start keeping
a journal, and I will keep one too.
We will respect the confidentiality
of each other's writing.**

"Science is a little bit like the air you breathe—it is everywhere."

Dwight D. Eisenhower

Science and technology are becoming more and more integrated into our world. We all have to keep up. Unfortunately, some adults are intimidated by science, and their children catch that fear.

Children aren't scared of science unless grown-ups make them afraid of it. To kids it's a game, just organized curiosity, and no one is more curious than a child.

One way or the other, your attitude will be contagious. Have fun together.

**I will teach my children to look at life
as a fascinating experiment in a world
full of discovery and wonder.**

"Work banishes those three great evils: boredom, vice, and poverty."

Voltaire

$\mathcal{K}$ids need to know that mothers (and fathers) work hard and do important things. Children should learn that there are lots of opportunities and choices in life. More doors are opening every day.

Mothers should also go to school with their children sometime. Parents need to know that kids work hard and do important things too!

I will show my children what I do at work, and I will find out what they do at school all day.

"The things we fear we bring to pass."

Elbert Hubbard

Keeping children safe in today's world is no easy task. Sometimes we exaggerate the dangers when we warn our children about legitimate threats. But children already fear lots of things—both real and imagined.

We want children to be wary of real dangers, not to be jumping at shadows. We want them to feel as safe as they can— safely. It's Mom's job to help them filter their fears through a screen of reality checks.

I will teach my children caution, not fear.

"Generations pass while some trees stand, and old families last not three oaks."

Sir Thomas Browne

*C*hildren have a natural affinity for trees. They are impressed by the size and shape of trees and how they change throughout the year. Trees are some of the first objects to appear in every child's drawings.

Kids just naturally love to play in, on, under, and around trees. Most adults can remember a favorite tree from childhood.

Do everything you can to give your child the same opportunities to be around trees that you had.

**I will plant a tree with my child.
It will be a gift to ourselves and our
legacy to future families.**

"Every walk is a sort of crusade."
Henry David Thoreau

*W*ise mothers know that walking and talking just seem to go together naturally. There's something about walking side by side with another human being that is conducive to conversation. It's also great exercise!

**Sometimes we will choose walking—
and talking—over riding.**

"The problems of adolescence have an infinite number of symptoms, but all have the same cause. The cause is preoccupation with self."

Linda and Richard Eyre

Teenagers are extremely self-sensitive, which makes them defensive, vulnerable, and fragile. The more quickly adolescents can get outside of themselves, the more quickly they can become responsible and mature young adults.

Mothers can help by getting their teenagers involved in social causes and service projects. It's better to be preoccupied with service than with self.

**I will try to get my teenagers
to think of others.**

"Work consists of whatever a body is obliged to do, and play consists of whatever a body is not obliged to do."

Mark Twain

*P*lay is a child's work. As they grow older, however, children need some real work to do. Work helps kids learn responsibility and accountability and gives them a sense of accomplishment. Play teaches lots of things, but it takes work to teach self-worth.

Don't shield your children from work. It can make them feel more grown up and a part of the real world.

I will find some tasks that are just right for my children. I will let them play, but I will let them work a little too.

"To maintain a joyful family requires much from both the parents and the children. Each member of the family has to become, in a special way, the servant of the others."

Pope John Paul II

A family is more than a group of people under one roof. Families work because all members give and give in. They look out for each other, and they serve each other's needs.

Being a good mother means being a good servant. Just remember, there's a difference between a servant and a slave.

I will serve my children's needs without doing everything for them.

"You can learn many things from children. How much patience you have, for instance."

Franklin P. Jones

You can't fast-forward childhood, and you can't make children mature and responsible overnight. If mothers are anything, they are patient.

Patience is every mother's secret weapon. It works. Most kids grow up OK.

**I will be patient with my children.
There's no rush for them to grow up.**

"Give yourself permission to be late sometimes. Life is for living, not scheduling."

Linus Mundy

$\mathcal{P}$romptness is a virtue, not a commandment. Don't miss something really important just to be on time. "Schedule" a little spontaneity in your child's life sometimes.

**I will remember that time
is not always of the essence.**

"Those who seek attention sometimes get more than they want."

Jerry Springer

Children thrive on attention. If they don't get it at home, they'll seek it elsewhere. If they don't get it for being good, they'll get it for being bad. Unfortunately, attention comes in many forms. Not all of them are pleasant.

Give your children the attention they need, or they'll get your attention in ways that may hurt you both. A mother's attention is a form of reward. It should be given freely and for good reasons.

I will make sure my children don't need to go elsewhere for the attention they deserve.

"Every man is a hero or an oracle to someone."
Ralph Waldo Emerson

*H*ave you ever wanted to be a heroine? You already are. Every mother is a heroine to her children—at least for a while.

It's not all fun. It's scary to be looked up to. It's both a great responsibility and a great opportunity.

You don't have to be perfect while you're up on the pedestal of motherhood. Just remember to ask yourself often whether your actions are setting the best possible example.

**I will be the kind of role model I've always
wanted for my children.**

"God will forgive me; that's his business."
Heinrich Heine

*E*very mother makes mistakes. Sometimes mothers inadvertently hurt their children. If this happens to you, don't give up and don't feel guilty. God will forgive you. Forgive yourself! Beating yourself up serves no one.

I'll remember that if I need punishing, someone else will have to do it.

"The thing is to be able to outlast the trends."
                                                    Paul Anka

*L*ife is more than the latest trend, but children can't look far enough ahead to see that. You can.

Use the benefit of your experience to show them that success does not come from jumping on every new bandwagon that comes along. Children love to hear stories about when their parents were young, and most of us have at least one that illustrates the perils of being a blind follower.

I will encourage my children to pursue their own goals and chart their own course.

"Who loves a garden still his Eden keeps."
                                        Amos Bronson Alcott

*C*hildren love dirt, pretty flowers, and making things happen. This makes them natural gardeners.

Gardening teaches responsibility, hard work, patience, satisfaction, joy, wonderment, and respect for beauty. These are lessons everyone needs.

Where else can kids learn how to make miracles and play in the mud at the same time?

**I will let my children plant a garden
of their own, even if it's just
flowerpots on a windowsill.**

"Lots of little children live at my house, and it shows."

Jane Welsey Bandsgaard

When you have children, it shows, They leave their mark on every aspect of your life. As you've learned, your house, your car, your wardrobe, your hair, and your makeup never look the same again once you've had children.

You've probably also learned not to fight it—it's a losing battle. Be proud to look like a mother.

**I'll keep in mind that being a mother
is always in fashion.**

"We must have a place where children can have a whole group of adults they can trust."

Margaret Mead

$\mathcal{F}$ ill your home with adults who will love and support your children. When it comes to caring adults, the more the merrier. Children can't have too many grown-ups in their corner.

For a child, home should be a haven of trust. When your children have a network of caring adults, they have almost all they need to grow up successfully.

I will invite grandparents and other close adults to visit our home often and become grown-up friends to my children.

"TV—chewing gum for the mind."
                    Frank Lloyd Wright

*T*elevision is a wondrous addition to a child's experience. It provides information, education, and entertainment (mostly entertainment). Like all media, however, it is incomplete.

A steady diet of television alone can lead to mental malnutrition. A child's media menu should include newspapers, magazines, books, movies, radio, recordings, theater, and concerts.

People can't live on chewing gum alone.

———————— ✤ ————————

**I will offer my children so many other
sources of learning and enjoyment that they
will turn off the TV on their own.**

"When I was a boy of fourteen, my father was so ignorant I could barely stand to have the man around. But when I got to be twenty-one, I was astonished at how much he had learned in seven years."

Mark Twain

*S*omewhere in their teens, children achieve perfect wisdom accompanied by an impatience with the dullness of adults—particularly parents.

Mothers expect this, tolerate it, and outlast it. Most teenagers eventually become normal human beings with only normal intelligence again within a few years. Wait it out!

I won't take my teenager's arrogance personally.

"All phone calls are obscene."

Karen Elizabeth Gordon

*T*eenagers bond with telephones. Talking on the phone is addictive for some kids. Like all addictions, it can upset the whole family.

Children need to know that telephones are intended as convenient instruments for communication, information, and fun. Talking on the phone, however, is not meant to be a way of life or a full-time occupation.

I will teach my children about phone rights and phone manners. (Alexander Graham Bell would approve.)

"The most widespread disease in the world is the inferiority complex."

Sterling Sill

*F*eeling inferior is a chronic, progressive, and crippling illness of epidemic proportions. No one has natural immunity. The disease is caught from other people and affects millions.

This is a case where the prevention and the cure are the same, and the most highly qualified specialist doesn't have to be a doctor. The simple inoculation is loving parents who set children up for success and praise them a lot.

I will boost my child's self-esteem through praise and positive reinforcement.

"Well begun is half done."

Aristotle

The best way to finish anything is to get a good start. The better the beginning, the easier the whole job.

Teach your children the power of getting off to a good start. It's another way of giving your children an edge.

People who hit the ground running usually finish ahead of the rest. Good beginnings make good endings.

**I will show my children how to get
a jump on success by expending extra
effort right from the start.**

"The family is a court of justice which never shuts down night or day."

De Chayal

*L*ife's not fair, but families should be. Every child should be able to expect fair treatment, a full hearing, and equal justice at home.

Good mothers see to it that everyone gets his or her day in court and no one receives cruel or unusual punishment.

In your house, insist on justice for all.

I will be a fair judge.

"Service is the rent we pay for living."
Marian Wright Edelman

$\mathscr{C}$hildren shouldn't grow up believing that life owes them anything. By nature children are good at taking. They have to learn to be good at giving.

It is our job, as adults, to teach them how to give back to the community.

We will plan a way that our family can work together to provide some service for the community.

"I'd help the homeless. And I would be sure that everyone has a rose."

Sixth-grader's essay

All of us, even little children, deserve to have something pretty (expensive or not) that belongs to us alone.

A thing of beauty all our own makes us feel special inside and helps fill up the empty places in our lives. Everyone should have a rose sometimes.

**I will give my child something beautiful
to cherish as a private treasure.**

"I suffer from an incurable disease—colour blindness."

Joost de Blank

We can't change who we are, but we can accept and take pride in who we are and where we came from. We all have heritages worth celebrating.

**My children and I will make a list of all
the things we have to be proud of.
We will keep the list.**

"Don't squat with your spurs on."

Billboard

We all do dumb things and hurt ourselves sometimes. We step on a rake, which then flips up and hits us in the head. We shut the car door on our own finger. We hold a match too long and burn our hand.

Kids need to know that doing dumb things doesn't make them dumb.

**I will tell my children about some
of the dumb things I've done in my life
so they won't feel stupid and alone
when it happens to them.**

What part of the word no *don't you understand?*

We owe our children discipline. Reasonable discipline defines acceptable behavior, sets standards, and guides action.

When grown-ups fail to provide discipline, send mixed messages, or make threats without following through, children become confused. They don't know what the rules are, so they behave without rules or make up their own. In adult society we call this *lawlessness*.

**I will be clear and consistent in my discipline.
I won't say no unless I mean no
and intend to enforce no.**

"On Mother's Day, there are no grown children. Everybody goes to Mom's."

Teresa Bloomingdale

$\mathcal{L}$ike Rodney Dangerfield, many mothers feel they don't get proper respect. The kids don't call often enough. They may forget birthdays or anniversaries or even Mother's Day.

Of course one reason your children do all of these terrible things is that they're busy doing what you taught them to do best—raising their own children.

This is the greatest tribute they can pay to you. Don't ask for a whole lot more.

I will enjoy watching my children raise their children, and I will take some credit for their success. That's respect!

"If you ruin your body, where will you live?"

Anon.

*O*n today's sideline society, many children and youth don't get proper exercise. Unfortunately, children are also notoriously bad eaters, and teenagers are even worse. Young people are not good to their bodies in America.

We're given many things, but only one body. We have to live in it all our life. We should nurture and maintain it as carefully as a sixteen-year-old looks after a first car. When Mom stays in good shape, the kids are more likely to stay fit too.

**I will start setting an example
of healthy living for my family.**

"In America, there are two classes of travel—first-class and with children."

Robert Benchley

Traveling with children is not without pain and discomfort; but it's the best way a family can see and learn about the world together.

Few parents have ever regretted the inconvenience or expense of a vacation with the kids. Traveling bonds family members in a way that isn't possible at home. Trips taken together build lifelong memories. The best time to travel with your children is always now!

This year we will plan a trip that all our family can enjoy together.

"Try to be a little kinder than necessary."
                                    Sir James Barrie

*C*hildren can be incredibly cruel or exceptionally kind.
Adults teach them how.

Kindness begets kindness. If we can teach our children to
be kind, they will live in a kinder world.

**My children and I will plan one act of
kindness that we can do together.**

"Eating words never gave me indigestion."
Winston Churchill

In the heat of the moment any mother might say something to her children that she shouldn't say, regrets, or doesn't mean. Pride and stubbornness should never stand in the way of apologizing for harsh or hurtful words.

--- ❧ ---

**When I say something I shouldn't,
I will promptly take back the words and
replace them with the kind of words adults
should say to children.**

"A man should be jailed for telling lies to the young."

Lillian Hellman

There's no greater letdown than a lie from a loved one. You owe your children the truth.

Even "little white lies" can be harmful to gullible and vulnerable little children. Being deceived never seems funny to them.

Before you fib in the name of shielding a child who is "too young" to hear the truth, ask yourself whom you're really trying to protect.

**I will tell my children the truth
no matter how difficult it may be.**

"Denial is not a river in Egypt."

AA adage

Denial is not a problem-solving process, but it is often a mother's first response to signs of trouble.

We never want to believe bad things can happen to the good people in our family or that our children can have serious problems with drugs, sex, or gangs. Nevertheless, every family will have trouble sooner or later.

Saying it isn't so won't solve problems. Confronting them head-on will. Good parents face facts and take action. Ask the difficult questions and talk about your fears and feelings.

I will confront my child if there are signs of trouble. After all, I'm the adult.

"For love includes anyone very dear to us. And he or she doesn't have to be present or lived with."

Marjorie Holmes

A mother's love isn't determined by proximity. When children grow up and leave home, they take it with them. The tether remains unbroken wherever they go.

There's no place a child can hide that a mother's love can't find. Be sure your children understand this fact of life. At some point it may comfort them on a cold night a long way from home.

I will let my children know that my love comes with a lifetime guarantee.

"Nature has always had more power than education."

Voltaire

All children (even city kids) need to spend some time in the real world—no blacktop, no plastic, no neon—the world as God made it. That's where tranquillity hangs out. Kids need to know that all bouquets don't come in spray cans.

Introduce your child to Mother Nature on her own turf. Stand quietly in a meadow together. It's called serenity.

**I will take my child
somewhere where we can't see cement.**

"Half the secret of resistance to disease is cleanliness; the other half is dirtiness."

Anon.

Kids are fascinated with mud. It's like a reconnection with the primal ooze. They love to jump in mud, squish it between their toes, and make it into pies.

Not all mothers are good mudders. Those who don't appreciate mud and want their children to avoid it really can't be blamed; cleanliness usually is a virtue. But this is a battle they're bound to lose.

Let your kids play in the mud. The mud will wash off, but the memories will last a lifetime.

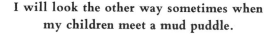

**I will look the other way sometimes when
my children meet a mud puddle.**

"Camps are the only places to learn the world in."
Philip Dormer Stanhope,
fourth Earl of Chesterfield

Going to camp can be a rite of passage for many kids. It teaches them rugged living and rugged independence at the same time. Campfires, camp food, and camp songs are the stuff memories are made of.

Of course, homesickness can be associated with camping, but it afflicts more parents than children.

Send your children to camp if you can. You'll both learn how to brave the elements without each other for a little while.

**I will make plans for my children
to go to camp. I will also plan how
I will welcome them back home.**

"Communication isn't measured by words."
Linus Mundy

*M*others can say a lot without uttering a word. Looks, gestures, actions, and body language speak out loud and clear to children. Kids can hear what you're not saying.

**I will watch what I'm saying
when I'm not talking.**

"Training is everything . . . cauliflower is nothing but cabbage with a college education."

Mark Twain

As much as you may love the idea of a liberal education, try to see that your children acquire some marketable skills along the way.

A broad education will help your children make a life, but specific training will help them make a living as well.

I will discuss with my children what kind of training they might want someday.

"At every moment you choose yourself."
                    Dag Hammarskjold

It's not fate. It's not the stars. It's us. We are what we make ourselves.

We can blame heredity or environment all we want, but the power to be what we want to be lies within each of us.

Living is choosing. Teach your children that they're in the driver's seat of their own lives. They can be almost anything. The choice is theirs.

**I will encourage my children
to choose to be their best.**

"No problem is too big to run away from."
Al Ries and Jack Trout

*B*eing a mother is a big job—sometimes too big! Every mother feels overwhelmed now and then. It's in the job description. It's also normal and nothing to feel ashamed about.

When things get to be too much, don't be afraid to walk away for a while. Even mothers deserve a break. Take yours and don't apologize for it.

I will recognize when hanging in there is doing no one any good.

"What is an adult? A child blown up by age."
Simone de Beauvoir

*B*eing a grown-up mother isn't all it's cracked up to be. It's a lot of thankless work and worry. It helps if you can keep a bit of the child alive somewhere inside of you.

Don't be too proud to be a little childish now and then. It's fun, and it helps keep you young. Besides, your kids will get a kick out of it.

**I will let the little kid inside me
out for a while every day.**

"The best way to keep children home is to make the home atmosphere pleasant—and let the air out of the tires."

Dorothy Parker

*N*o matter what a mother does, there comes a time when children will prefer to be someplace other than at home. It's nothing personal. It means your kids are becoming more mature and independent.

Don't fight it. That is what you've been working for. Besides, the quiet may do you some good.

Just be sure your children know that they can always stay home or come home whenever they want or need to.

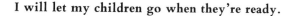

I will let my children go when they're ready.

"Say it with flowers."

Patrick O'Keefe

Mothers and children don't spend enough time with flowers. Kids live by their senses. They are enthralled by the beauty, the fragrance, and the delicate touch of flowers. Children have time to stop and smell the roses. Surround your children with lots of flowers when they are small.

Later on, the memories, the images, and the magic of flowers will provide a lifetime of pleasure.

I will visit a flower garden with my children.

"Add up what you have, and you'll find that you won't sell them for all the gold in the world."

Dale Carnegie

$\mathcal{K}$ids cost a lot. When budgets are stretched to the limit, some parents fantasize about what life might have been like without children. Some even wonder if they made the right investment. In her heart, every mother knows the answer is yes!

Children are a special treasure. No matter how much they cost, they're always worth more. Family is better than fortune. In fact, family is fortune. That's why mothers are richer than most folks.

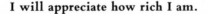

I will appreciate how rich I am.

"The family is the nucleus of civilization."
Will and Ariel Durant

Politicians are beginning to realize anew that civil society begins and ends with family. There are all kinds of families, and they can all work. Nothing can take their place.

In a nation run amok, hope can be rebuilt only one family at a time.

Mothers have known this all along.

**I will teach my children
that we are all something with family.**

"The value of marriage is not that adults produce children but that children produce adults."

Peter DeVries

$\mathcal{N}$othing makes a woman grow up quicker than becoming a mother. Children will do that to you. Kids make grown-ups out of ordinary people.

Congratulate yourself for being the kind of adult your child needs.

**I will take pride in being the
adult parent my children deserve.**

"I think patriotism is like charity; it begins at home."

Henry James

Grown-ups continuously complain about our government and our country. We criticize it a lot because we can. That's the beauty of America.

Kids won't know we love our country unless we tell them. It's our duty to teach our children that patriotism isn't corny. Loyalty and love of country never go out of style.

America doesn't always work perfectly, but it works better for raising families than anyplace else in the world. Let your kids in on the secret.

I will tell my child how I really feel about our country. If we don't have one, we'll buy an American flag and display it proudly.

"But spare your country's flag."
John Greenleaf Whittier

Flags appeal to children of all ages. They're fun to look at and fun to wave. Of course, flags are more than artwork or playthings. They have meaning, symbolism, and significance. People die for them.

Teach your children what our flag stands for and why we respect it. It's an important part of their culture too.

---------------- ----------------

**We will fly our country's flag
and pledge our allegiance to it.**

"The buck stops here."

Harry Truman

We all wish someone else would solve our problems. It doesn't work that way. Washington doesn't solve kids' problems. Families do.

When it comes to raising our children, it's no one else's job. It's ours. If the TV needs turning off, do it. That's what mothers are for.

**I will do what needs to be done
to raise my children and not wait for
someone else to handle it.**

"Time is but the stream I go a-fishing in."
Henry David Thoreau

There's a difference between kid time and mother time. To mothers, childhood and adolescence always go by too fast.

It's not that way for kids. To a child, some minutes are like hours, and a school year is forever.

Children probably have a better attitude about time than adults do. Who's to say what reality is?

Allow your children to live in their own time. They'll be on adult time soon enough.

I will live with the fact that my children live in a different time zone.

"Most people use only 40 percent of their potential."
Robert Kerlin

*M*ost children and adults are underachievers. They use less than one-half of their true potential. The majority of people reach what they think is their natural plateau and quit. They can do better.

If your children can achieve at near capacity, they will be light-years ahead of the pack. The secret is in the trying. People who continually strive are the ones who thrive.

Teach your children to stretch and to try to do more than they think they can do. Urge them to reach—and keep reaching! That's what winners do!

***

**I will challenge my children to keep trying.
I don't want them to settle for
what's comfortable.**

*"It's but little good you'll do a-watering the last
year's crops."*

George Eliot

It's OK to enjoy memories or revisit the past occasionally,
but don't make a home there. It's hard to move ahead if
you're always looking backward.

Whatever you do with the past won't change anything for
today or tomorrow. Learn from past mistakes and reflect on
what worked for you yesterday. Then get on with your life.

Teach your children to do the same. They will live in the
future, so they should focus their attention forward.

**I will model living for today and planning
for tomorrow, not dwelling on yesterday.**

"Never confuse motion with action."

Ernest Hemingway

$\mathcal{S}$ome mothers are hyperactive and proud of it. They think motherhood demands constant frenzy. They unceasingly flit from one thing to another. They're always busy. But how much do they accomplish?

Often very little. Step back and compare your effort with the results. You don't have to look busy every second to prove you're trying. Slow down and set priorities.

A hyper mother raises hyper kids.

**I'll stop being so busy
and get something done.**

"Violence is the repartee of the illiterate."

Alan Brien

Violence is an unacceptable parenting skill. Mothers influence lives and change the world—all without violence.

Show your kids how you get things done without beating up on people. Avoiding violence isn't an act of cowardice. Nobody calls a mother "chicken."

The lesson of nonviolence is a lesson in living a longer, better life.

I will show my children how to use reason and compromise to win battles without force or violence.

"Life is a bundle of little things."
                                    Oliver Wendell Holmes

eing a good mother isn't about grandiose actions or earthshaking events. It's about doing lots of little things that have to be done when they have to be done.

If you take care of all the little things, the big things will fall into place. In motherhood the whole is greater than the sum of its parts.

**I will pay attention to details
and take care of today's business today.**

"Always quit on a high note."
Maryann and Carl Elkins

*K*ids overdo things. Too many treats. Too much TV. Too much Nintendo. By themselves, children won't control excesses. Mothers have to.

When things are overdone, they lose their appeal. There's a difference between satisfaction and saturation.

It's better to quit while things are going well and still enjoyable so kids will look forward to a next time. Good memories are built by quitting while you're ahead.

**I will stop my children
before they overdo things.**

"You can do anything with children if you only play with them."

Otto von Bismarck

Sometimes we think we're too busy to play with our children. We believe playing is just for kids. We're mistaken.

Play is an entrée into a child's world. It bonds, builds rapport, and bolsters communication. Playing together makes adult and child equal for the moment.

Children are more willing to play your games if you play theirs. It's another way of showing you care. Besides, it's fun.

**I will set aside at least thirty minutes a day
to play with my child.**

"The toast always lands jelly-side down."
                                        Suzann Ledbetter

Murphy must have been a mother, because "Murphy's Law" is what parenting is all about. Mishaps and screwups are part of the daily routine for mothers. If you get bored when things go too smoothly, try raising a child.

Something is likely to go wrong every day when children are in the house. You might as well expect it and take it in stride.

**I will plan on something going wrong every
day and will look for the humor in it.
(It's bound to be there.)**

"I think a little bit of nurse lurks in every woman."
Marjorie Holmes

"Dr. Mom" is not an invention. It's a reality. Mothers know a lot about caring for sick children and making little hurts feel better. Mostly they know how vulnerable a sick child feels and how much comfort some tenderness can provide.

A mother's love can be medicinal.

—————— ——————

**I'll make sure my children know
they don't have to be too brave around me
when they're ill or hurt.**

"My grandfather always said that living is like licking honey off a thorn."

Louis Adamic

Mothers are natural philosophers. They know that raising children is always a bittersweet experience.

Children will hurt you sometimes while giving you untold joy at others. Raising a family isn't "happiness ever after." It's reality, with its ups and downs. Mothers take lots of lumps just like everyone else.

I will teach my children to take the bad with the good and to roll with the punches.

"You can observe a lot just by watching."

Yogi Berra

*C*hildren act out their feelings and emotions. Watching them at play with friends or on their own is a good way to gauge their moods and find out what's really on their minds. Often you can find out more from a little observation than from a lot of questioning.

Smart mothers learn to read their children by watching them when they don't know they're under observation.

I will try to get closer to my children by watching them from a distance.

"We learn from experience. A man never wakes his second baby just to see it smile."

Grace Williams

Since there's no user's manual, part of parenting is trial and error. The first child is always the subject of experimentation. Mistakes will be made. Fortunately, our babies don't recognize them and don't hold grudges.

One of the secrets of successful motherhood is to avoid agonizing when you do something wrong and to learn from the experience.

I'll try not to make the same mistake twice.

"Callithump: a noisy boisterous band or parade."
Merriam Webster's Collegiate Dictionary

*E*verybody loves a parade—especially kids. Parades are celebrations on foot, full of sights, sounds, and fun. No one can feel down or depressed at a parade.

Take your children to see a parade. Better yet, have one in your own neighborhood.

**I will plan a parade showcasing
all the kids on the block.**

"I am not obliged to know everything."

Maya Angelou

The whole world expects a lot of mothers. Sometimes mothers expect even more of themselves.

All that's really required is that mothers love their children and do their best. They don't have to do everything or know everything.

I will not expect too much of myself.

*"When I see the Ten Most Wanted Lists, I always
have this thought: If we'd made them feel wanted
earlier, they wouldn't be wanted now."*

Eddie Cantor

We can't give our children everything, but we can give them a sense of being welcome in this world.

Children want to be wanted more than anything else. Our children tell us they love us, yet we still feel taken for granted at times. It works both ways.

We all need to hear how important we are to those we love. Children who feel unwanted never quite feel they belong as adults.

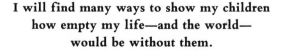

**I will find many ways to show my children
how empty my life—and the world—
would be without them.**

145

"No one is wise enough by himself."
                        Titus Maccius Plautus

*N*o parents know everything or can do everything by themselves. None of us has a monopoly on wisdom. Even single mothers don't have to raise their children in total isolation. We all need a third-party point of view sometimes.

Don't be afraid to ask for assistance or advice. Seeking help isn't a sign of weakness.

Get all the second opinions you want and then do what you think is right. That's good parenting.

I will ask for advice when I want it, but I'll always reserve the right not to follow it.

"Mornings are special."

Marjorie Holmes

*M*ornings are the freshest part of the day. Everything is new; nothing's been spoiled yet. Morning moments should be enjoyed.

In many households, however, mornings are a madhouse. Everyone is hurried and hassled and gets off to a frantic start. A bad beginning sets the tone for the entire day.

If we managed our mornings better, the rest of our lives might go better too.

I'll rise a little earlier so I'll have time to enjoy the morning with my child.

"Problems are messages."

Shakti Gawain

$\mathcal{F}$amily problems don't just spring up by magic. They are caused. They are results connected to other events in our lives. When serious problems between parents and children keep recurring, it usually means that something in the family system isn't working.

When this happens, it's not enough to resolve the immediate situation. Look for the underlying cause. Fix the system, not just the symptom.

I won't settle for quick fixes. I'll try to figure out why we're having problems and work on long-term solutions.

"When television is bad, nothing is worse."
Newton Norman Minow

*M*others can't keep kids from watching TV. They can, however, set limits, influence choices, and talk about what's good and bad on television.

Television is intended as a resource for entertainment and information. It's not designed to be a child's only education or to be a full-time baby-sitter. Know when to turn it off.

**I'll teach my child that we can
use television without letting it use us.**

"Do not be breakin' a shin on a stool that's not in your way."

Irish proverb

Some mothers get nervous when things go too smoothly. Good fortune scares them. They court calamity because they count on it.

Enjoy the good times (you deserve them). There will be plenty of bad times to worry about later.

--------------- ---------------

**I won't go looking for
trouble where there isn't any.**

150

"The important thing is not to stop questioning."
                              Albert Einstein

As any mother of a three-year-old can attest, children's queries can be exhausting. Just when you think you've answered every possible question on a subject, here comes that "Why?" again.

Don't despair. Remember that curiosity is an expression of intelligence. No one would want to stifle a child's eagerness to discover and learn.

Inevitably your own fountain of knowledge will run dry, however, so be sure you have other resources at hand.

**I will teach my children how to answer
their own questions by making books and
other resources available to them.**

*"Technology . . . the knack of so arranging the world
that we don't have to experience it."*

Max Frisch

*M*odern technology can expand human potential or
dehumanize society. It's our choice.

Children must master today's technology to succeed in life.
It's our job, however, to help them avoid becoming dependent
on CD-ROM, interactive videos, or virtual reality to the exclu-
sion of having direct experience. We don't want our kids to
grow up hiding behind computers. Life is more than a series of
simulations.

**I will help my children balance
technological skills with human skills.**

"Relationships can't be built by keeping score."

Anon.

*C*hildren shouldn't be used as pawns in their parents' power plays. Raising a child isn't a game of one-upmanship. It's not about competing or using a child to get even with a spouse. Parenting doesn't have winners or losers.

In real families, everyone wins, and no one keeps score.

I won't play games with family relationships.

"Parents are the bones on which children sharpen their teeth."

Peter Ustinov

Kids have to beat up on their parents. It's part of growing up and learning to be independent. Sooner or later your child will test you, resist you, and fight to pull away. Most children become defensive and/or argumentative during adolescence.

Mothers should expect challenges and not be hurt by them. That's why mothers need to have thick hides.

**I won't take my child's
resisting authority personally.**

"Trust your gut. It doesn't know how to lie."
                                          Elvis Presley

*M*other's intuition is a gut feeling that something is true or right despite logical evidence to the contrary. It's spooky, but it works.

When you're getting mixed messages from your head and your heart, go with your heart.

Don't fight your intuition or try to explain it. Just act on it and be thankful for the gift.

———————— ————————

**I'll trust my gut feelings
and follow my instincts.**

"Always set a place in life for the unexpected guest."

Anon.

A mother's life is full of surprises. That's what makes it interesting and exciting. If you can't stand having your routines destroyed and your life turned upside down without notice, you probably shouldn't be in the mother business.

The secret of survival is to expect the unexpected. Have fun even though you're not always in control.

**I will go with the flow
and not let surprises disconcert me.**

"It's a pity that men and women forget they have been children. Parents are apt to be foreigners to their sons and daughters."

George William Curtis

Sometimes as parents we view our children as little adults. We lose patience when they don't respond to our compelling logic. We're embarrassed by their childish behavior. We wish they'd act more grown up. We don't understand what's wrong with them.

Actually, it shouldn't be that hard for adults to understand children. We've been where they are. They haven't been where we are.

I'll remember what it was like to be a kid so I won't expect too much.

"Adults always have to make a point."

Anon.

We all take our work too seriously sometimes. Mothers are especially susceptible—motherhood is, after all, a serious business. But you shouldn't feel compelled to constantly inform, instruct, or inspire.

There's no law that says mothers always have to make a point. Sometimes it's better to play the less demanding role of ordinary person than of mother.

I won't have an agenda for every moment.

"Advertising is legalized lying."

H. G. Wells

TV advertisers love kids. They delight in planting big ideas in little heads about how to spend Mom and Dad's money. It's easy to sell to children because they believe what they see or hear.

That's why mothers and fathers have to enforce truth in advertising. Children need to learn that life isn't a commercial. The world isn't really made up exclusively of beautiful people with hard bellies and no pimples.

Advertising should come with a warning label for kids.

**I will help my children compare
what they see in advertising
with what they see in real life.**

159

"Parenting is no joke."

Harlem Globetrotters' spokesperson
for "male responsibility"

Too many young males today have a false sense of what it means to have a baby. They don't take parenting seriously. They just don't get it. They don't take responsibility, and they often take off. This should be unacceptable in a nation that cherishes its children.

Today's mothers need to educate tomorrow's parents (especially boys) about their responsibilities. At the very least, tomorrow's children deserve parents who are willing to raise them.

**I will talk to my children about the
responsibility of being a mother or father.**

"What happens around a dinner table when a family gathers at early evening? The answer is 'More than you know.'"

Marianne Williamson

It's always surprising what images people carry from childhood to adulthood. Little things can make big impressions. What seems ordinary to adults may be monumental to a child. An adult's offhand comment can become a child's lifetime memory.

Mothers and other adults should be on guard around children. Remember, there's a lot more going on than you realize.

**I will remember that
little eyes are watching me.**

"Normal adolescence is sometimes very abnormal."
Leigh Abrahamson

*M*any mothers are caught by surprise when their children hit the turbulent teens. All of a sudden their innocent children become rebellious youths who dress weirdly and speak in tongues.

Expect a little strange behavior during adolescence. It's part of growing up. Don't panic. Teenagism is a temporary disease.

No matter how difficult your teenager may be, there's an adult in there somewhere trying to get out. Be patient.

**I will remember that
adolescence isn't forever.**

"Everyone loves an opening night."
   Maryann and Carl Elkins

heater is so much like child's play that children make a natural audience. To kids, all of life is a production. Watching a play is just like looking in the mirror.

The living bond between actor and audience enables plays to instruct, inspire, and entertain children more personally than any other medium. Plays give children a different way of looking at their world.

**We will make plans
to attend a children's play.**

*"Consider the little mouse, how sagacious an animal
it is which never entrusts its life to one hole only."*
                                    Titus Maccius Plautus

When a baby is born, the world is full of possibilities. From then on, life is a series of closed or closing doors.

Don't let your children narrow their interests too soon. Help them keep their options open. Broaden their horizons as much as possible for as long as possible.

Mothers should be door openers, not door closers.

**I will help my child
see multiple possibilities.**

"A child should not be denied a balloon because an adult knows that sooner or later it will burst."

Marcelion Cox

Temporary pleasures are better than no pleasures at all. Just because a sensation won't last is no reason to keep a child from experiencing it.

Kids can handle a little disappointment. They'll soon get over a popped balloon. The balloon may burst, but the memory will be floating around a long time.

I will let my child enjoy the moment even though I know it won't last.

"Momsense is language or ideas intelligible only to mothers."

Teresa Bloomingdale

Mothers are magic. They see things, hear things, and know things that others don't. Mothers have special senses, perceptions, sensitivities, and intuitions. They have to. It's the way they raise children without a user's manual.

Part of being a mother is ESP. Never underestimate its power or question its validity.

**I will trust my "momsense"
to help raise my children.**

"Blest be the man who first invented sleep."
Miguel de Cervantes

hildren can do without a lot of things, but sleep isn't one of them. Rest is essential to revitalize mind, body, and spirit. Children need to get sleep, but they don't always welcome it.

It's the parents' responsibility to establish a regular routine for bedtime and a proper schedule of waking and sleeping. Children won't do it on their own.

Bedtime shouldn't be a debate tournament or a battle-ground. It should be as natural and unequivocal as sundown.

Sleep isn't negotiable.

**I will be firm and consistent
about my child's bedtime.**

"Animals are nothing but the forms of our virtues and vices, wandering before our eyes."

Victor Hugo

Children don't own pets. They're equals. To a child, a pet can be a partner, a playmate, a confidant, and a best pal. A child with a close pet is never friendless or lonely.

Animals have a civilizing effect on people. Bring one into your household. Your child will thank you for it.

I will talk to my children about what kind of pet would best suit our family. We will choose one together.

"Don't rescue kids from losing."

Dr. Sylvia Rimm

All mothers want to protect their children, sometimes too much. It's human nature to want to protect children from losing, but that's not always what's best for them.

We can all learn from losing. We learn that no one wins all the time. We learn what it takes to win. We learn that it's no fun to lose but it's not the end of the world either.

Let your children lose sometimes, but help them understand that losing isn't forever.

**I will let my child know that there's a
difference between losing and being a loser.**

"A good laugh is sunshine in the house."
William Makepeace Thackeray

*L*aughter adds sparkle to life. It breaks the tension and tedium of family living and makes life more fun. As grown-ups we remember the laughs of childhood more than the tears.

Make laughing a habit. Everyone would rather live in a house with laughter in it.

I will be sure to laugh
***with* my children and *at* myself.**

"Libraries can be of indispensable service in lifting the dead weight of poverty and ignorance."

Frances Keppel

*F*ew things are free these days. Public libraries still are. To children, a library can be like a toy store for the mind and spirit. Where else can you find Dr. Seuss and Dr. Zhivago waiting for you under one roof?

Libraries are too good a deal for mothers to miss out on. Turn your child loose with a library card often.

We will visit our public library regularly.

"A man finds out what is meant by a spitting image when he tries to feed cereal to his infant."

Imogene Frey

In some families food time is fight time. Mother and child are constantly engaged in a power struggle over what and how much to eat. Mealtime becomes a showdown.

Kids will eat when they're hungry and quit when they're full. There's not much a mother can do about that.

Waging war over a piece of broccoli is hardly worthwhile. Relaxed meals are best for everyone. If you're going to battle with your child over every meal, you'll lose.

**I will not make my child's
eating habits a major issue.**

"Children are natural poets."

Jane Welsey Bandsgaard

*C*hildren love to play with sounds and meanings. Using words in new and different ways amuses them, and rhyming is a favorite game.

Poetry doesn't scare children off. It's fun for them. Reading and writing poetry helps them learn about language and about life at the same time.

**I will share some favorite poems
with my children and encourage them
to make up some of their own.**

"To lengthen thy life, lessen thy meals."
Benjamin Franklin

*O*f mothers have one universal flaw, it's that they try to feed their children too much. In many families the surest way to insult Mom is not to eat everything she cooks. It lasts a lifetime.

In today's world eating right means eating light. It's time for mothers to back off from the bake-off. If you feed your kids less, you may be able to feed them a lot longer.

I will feed my children well, but I won't take uneaten portions as a personal affront.

"Learn some and think some and draw and paint and sing and dance and play and work every day some."
Robert Fulghum

The formula for a happy childhood is variety and balance. Doing lots of interesting things makes interesting children. All kids need a balance of activities. Infancy and childhood are no time for specialization.

Part of a mother's job is to broker activities so that children have a lot of different things to do to develop all facets of themselves. Raising children is a lot like managing a three-ring circus. That's the fun of it.

**I will see that my children have a balance
of physical, mental, and social activities.**

"It's a wise father who knows his own son."
William Shakespeare

others may still be the primary caregivers, but they don't have a monopoly on child raising. A team of parents can give a child twice the love and two hearts for the price of one.

Mothers are magic, but fathers are special too. Make room for Daddy in your child's life. Your whole family will be stronger for it.

I will involve Dad as much as possible in raising our children.

"What's the salvation of the movies? I say, run 'em backwards. It can't hurt and it's worth a try."

Will Rogers

*M*ovies are larger than life. The big screen has a powerful influence on kids. When movies are good, they're very good. When they're bad—watch out!

Enjoy good movies with your children. (While you're at it, teach them some movie manners so others can enjoy the show too.) Going to the movies can be a great family event.

We will pick out a movie our whole family can enjoy. At the same time, I will teach my children what the movie rating system means and why it is needed.

"If I do not read, nobody will."

Ralph Waldo Emerson

*R*eading is contagious. If your children see you reading, they are more apt to read themselves. There's no greater legacy a mother can leave than a love of reading.

Books are a way to multiply knowledge and experience without ever leaving home. Let your kids in on the secret.

———— ⚜ ————

I will make sure my children see me reading, and I will read to them often, even after they learn to read themselves.

"I use not only all the brains I have, but all the brains I can borrow."

Woodrow Wilson

When a family problem occurs, there's no law that says Mother has to solve it by herself. Mothers don't have a corner on the wisdom market.

Let everyone in on the action. If you tap into the best thinking of the whole family, you're likely to come up with a better answer.

If everyone is part of the problem solving, no one can complain about the solution.

**I will share family problems,
and we will solve them together.**

"Exercise and temperance can preserve something of our early strength even in old age."

Cicero

Too many American children are overweight and out of shape. Adults aren't the only ones who can be couch potatoes. Nintendo and TV don't constitute a workout program.

A fit life begins with a fit body. See that your child gets plenty of exercise.

---- ----

**I will do some aerobic exercises
with my children.**

"One friend in a lifetime is much; two are many; three are hardly possible."

Henry Brooks Adams

All kids want friends. The trouble is that most want friendships to just "happen" to them. They don't want to work at them.

Friendship is always a dividend earned by investing in another person. It has to be a two-way street. People with the most friends know how to be best friends.

Teach your children what it takes to be a friend and to have a friend. They will need good friends, as well as good parents, all their lives.

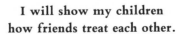

**I will show my children
how friends treat each other.**

"Democracy is not a spectator sport."
                              Marian Wright Edelman

*I*f democracy ever dies, it will be by default. It can fail only if enough people quit—quit participating, quit voting, quit speaking out, quit paying attention, and quit caring.

Teach your children not to be quitters. Individuals *can* make a difference. There is no better environment for raising families than a democracy.

**I will volunteer to work for
a political candidate or cause of my choice
and tell my children why.**

*"There are a hundred ways to overcome an obstacle
and one sure way not to—self-pity."*

Dale Dauten

Kids are good at feeling sorry for themselves. They learn it from adults.

Unfortunately, self-pity doesn't work for either children or grown-ups. It's nonproductive and often makes things worse.

Teach your children to talk things out or take some positive action rather than feeling sorry for themselves.

**I will teach my children that if you feel sorry
for yourself no one else will.**

*"Humor is a serious thing. I like to think of it as
one of our greatest and earliest natural resources,
which must be preserved at all costs."*

James Thurber

Humor is a mother's magic. It can turn frustration into
amusement and make tears disappear.

Humor is the balm that makes life bearable. It helps us get
through the bad times and make the most of the good times.
Don't leave home without it.

Without humor, families fail.

**I will keep my sense of humor
by sharing it with others.**

"Thinking is the hardest work there is, which is the probable reason why so few engage in it."

Henry Ford

Most people think only older kids with big IQs can learn higher-level thinking skills. The truth is that children of all ages and ability levels can learn how to think. Too often adults don't give them the tools.

It doesn't have to be that way at your house. Start by asking your children open-ended questions and giving them problems to solve. The more they practice thinking, the better they'll get. It's worth the effort. The world needs more thinking people.

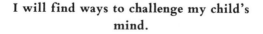

I will find ways to challenge my child's mind.

*"It is safe to say that no man ever went wrong,
morally or mentally, while listening to a symphony."*

Anon.

Every age has its own music. It defines the generation gap.

Unless you're deaf, you won't be able to escape your children's music. It's only fair, then, that they be exposed to some of yours.

Introduce your children to classical music. It cuts across generations and outlasts the sounds of the day.

Your children will secretly thank you for the experience—either now or later on.

———————— ❧ ————————

I will take my child to a symphony concert.

"I have found the best way to give advice to your children is to find out what they want and then advise them to do it."

Harry Truman

As children grow older, parental advice loses its luster. Eventually what children need most is support for the answers they already have and the advice they've already given themselves.

Your children won't always listen to you, but you can help them listen to themselves. Your kids will always follow your advice if they think it's their idea.

I will quit giving my children unwanted advice and start urging them to listen to their own inner voices.

"To my way of thinking there's something wrong, or missing, with any person who hasn't got a soft spot in their hearts for an animal of some kind."

Will James

*K*ids and animals go together. Children of all ages are naturally curious about animals and love to be around them. They learn a lot about how nature works by watching animals. In fact many animals aren't bad role models for humans.

Introduce your children to as many different kinds of animals as possible. People who get along well with animals seem to get along better with people too.

**I will make the local zoo
one of our regular outings.**

"Much of the world's work is done by men who do not feel quite well."

John Galbraith

Children are good at using illness as an excuse. It's a slick way to avoid unpleasantness and get some sympathy at the same time.

If all the children who said they didn't feel well stayed home from school, nobody would ever graduate. Sometimes children are so convincing that they don't know themselves whether they're really sick until their mother tells them.

Children need to know that people don't have to feel perfect to be good enough to get the job done.

———————— ✃ ————————

I will be a shrewd diagnostician, able to tell the difference between malady and mischief.

"Keep a stiff upper lip."

Phoebe Cary

When a crisis strikes and everyone is rattled, somebody
has to take charge and keep cool. That somebody is
often Mother.

Going to pieces won't put things back together. In an
emergency, grit your teeth, stay calm, and take care of business
first. You can fall apart later.

I will be ready to handle emergencies.

"Life's dearest perfumes aren't kept in expensive bottles on a dressing table."

Marjorie Holmes

The things that excite our senses most aren't manufactured. They're found in nature.

Teach your children to use all of their senses to savor the world's natural sights, sounds, and smells. These can't be bought, and they can't be bottled. They're nature's gifts to all of us, and they last a lifetime.

**I will take time
to smell the roses with my child.**

"The definition of insanity is the repetition of the same action expecting different results."

John Larroquette

*S*ometimes we get stuck on a certain approach or form of discipline even though it is unsuccessful with our children. It's crazy to keep doing the same thing over and over with no results.

No matter what Dr. Spock or any other authority says, if something doesn't work with your kids, drop it and try something else.

Good parenting is doing what works!

**When one technique doesn't work,
I'll have another at hand to try.**

"For teachers old age arrives every year."
                                        Tracy Kidder

*R*espect (and sympathize with) teachers. Nobody chooses to be a teacher because he or she doesn't like children and wants to do them harm.

Teachers and mothers should never be in competition. They have the same goals. The classroom is an extension of the home.

Give your child's teacher your trust and your support. A mother and a teacher working together can be an awesome force for good in a child's life.

**I will call my child's teacher
to express my approval and offer my help.**

"You know how to whistle, don't you? You just put your lips together and blow."

Lauren Bacall

Whistling is one of life's joyous sounds. Kids are absorbed by whistling. They love to learn how to do it. Many spend hours blowing and puckering to master the art.

Encourage your children to whistle. It can give them a lift whenever they need it. It's hard to whistle and be unhappy at the same time.

I will teach my children to whistle.

"Children have never been very good at listening to their elders, but they have never failed to imitate them."

James Baldwin

*M*others teach children more by how they live than by what they say (even though most mothers say a lot). You can't talk children into doing right. You have to show them how to do it.

**I will be a good model
for my child to imitate.**

"Boys do not grow up gradually. They move forward in spurts."

Cyril Connolly

It's easy to become too concerned about your children's day-by-day development, especially when they're babies and especially with your first. You can drive yourself crazy worrying that your child isn't growing as fast as the neighbor kid or keeping up with what the "charts" say is average. Or you can recognize that your child is thriving and appreciate his or her uniqueness.

It's amazing how much growth occurs when you're not paying attention. Growing up seems to occur all of a sudden.

**I will relax, watch, and wait
for my child to grow up.**

"Civility costs nothing."

Proverb

It doesn't take any more time or effort to be respectful and polite to people than it does to be vulgar and crude. Being nice isn't being weak. It's part of being human—a cut above the brute.

Teach your children to be civil. It will make them better people and add to a better world. Civility is a mark of true civilization.

I will insist on civility from my children.
Respect is one of those things
you get by giving it away.

"We must just KBO [Keep Buggering On]."
                                        Winston Churchill

*P*art of motherhood is simply "keeping on going." Life can be mean. Chaos isn't uncommon. But successful mothers don't quit, don't give up, and don't back off.

The 3 *p*s of parenting are patience, persistence, and perseverance. Practice these and you'll surprise yourself with decent, grown children before you know it.

**When things get tough,
I will just keep on going!**

"Hurry! I never hurry. I have no time to hurry."
Igor Stravinsky

*T*oo many mothers and too many children are too hurried and hassled. It doesn't have to be that way.

There's more to living than haste. Your life will take the same amount of time whether you race through it or meander along the way. Sometimes meandering is better.

All of life shouldn't be rock and roll. Save time for a waltz now and then.

I will lift up on the pedal of life a little.

"A smart mother often makes a better diagnosis than a dumb doctor."

August Bier

*M*others aren't doctors, but they're good substitutes. Most mothers can tell whether their child is really ill or just faking it. Likewise, most mothers can sense whether or not a condition is serious.

Use your own common sense in caring for your children. You know them better than anyone.

I'll trust my instincts to determine when a doctor is needed rather than calling the doctor for every sniffle.

"Let no one ignorant of mathematics enter here."

Plato

Mathematics is the language of logic. Everyone needs to be fluent, not just to survive in our technological society but also to get through everyday life.

Whether they know it or not, children who like music or puzzles or secret codes—who doesn't?—already like math. So how do children end up with math phobia? They inherit it from their parents!

Show your kids that you too think math is fun.

---　✧　---

**I will play number games with my children.
We may do some math puzzles too.**

"Pediatricians eat because children don't."

Meyer A. Peristein

Kids who eat right feel right—and do better in school and in life. Good nutrition is nature's secret for successful living. There is life after junk food.

Mothers (and fathers) don't just make dinner. They build lifelong eating habits. Fortunately, it doesn't cost any more to serve healthful meals. Teach your children to eat a well-balanced diet and you will give them a jump start on each day of the rest of their lives.

**I will teach my children all I know
about good nutrition so they will make
sound choices on their own.**

"The best time not to do drugs or alcohol is the first time."

Mickey Mantle

*I*t's never too early to start explaining to your children the dangers of drug use and abuse.

Just remember, there's a difference between explaining and sermonizing. Kids have a natural immunity to sermons.

I will talk to my children about the high costs of getting high and remind them of real-world examples we all know about.

"Who dares, wins."
Motto of the British Special Air Service regiment

 ou may not want your children to be daredevils, but you should want them to be risk takers. Timidity is the antithesis of accomplishment. That's why always playing it safe can be dangerous.

The meek may inherit the earth, but it's going to take a long time. Speed up the process by encouraging your children to try new things and to take a chance now and then. It will expand their horizons and enrich their lives.

I will urge my children to dare to live.

"Parents are strange . . . for their age."

Amanda Vail

*M*others should expect that their children will think them weird. Part of being a good mother is acting strange. It's called the generation gap. It's OK, because your kids will seem bizarre to you too.

Eventually you'll both appear normal to each other again. Rivers that part usually flow back together again downstream a way.

I will take pride in my weirdness.
It shows I'm a typical mother.

"A photograph is not only an image; it is also a trace, something directly stenciled off the real, like a footprint."

Susan Sontag

Kids love looking at photographs—of themselves, their pets, their family, their friends, their vacations—over and over again.

Children also love to take pictures. Kids and cameras make lasting memories.

**I will make sure my child has some time
behind the camera as well as in front of it.**

"You can't step into the same river twice."

Heracleitus

In raising children, the "teachable moment" may occur only once. The right time may never come by again.

You can't "freeze-frame" life and come back to it when you're ready. It's constantly changing.

If now seems like the time to make a point, teach a lesson, or share a special thought, do it.

I won't wait for second chances.

"Poverty is not a crime."

Proverb

*O*n our acquisitive age, it's hardly surprising when a child looks down on someone who doesn't wear the latest fashions or have the newest toys. Children need to be taught that appearances are not everything. All kinds of people are poor, just as all kinds are rich.

Encourage your children to judge others based on what's inside. Show them that economic status does not equal character, that poverty is a state, not a sin. The world doesn't need a new generation of snobs.

**I will teach my children to enjoy
people for who they are, not what they have.**

"They know enough who know how to learn."
Henry Brooks Adams

In today's world information is changing too fast for anyone to own it. New knowledge is being created constantly. Even history is being rewritten with new discoveries.

The greatest service you and your schools can provide your children is to teach them how to access information, how to organize it, and how to present it. These skills are worth an infinity of memorized facts.

Teach your children how to learn first and worry about what they will learn later.

**I will ask my children's teachers how I can
help improve their learning skills.**

"Throw dirt enough and some will stick."

Proverb

ad-mouthing other people is a sorry excuse for conversation. Without guidance, children can be the worst offenders. Kids learn to gossip from grown-ups. They need to understand that words can hurt feelings, reputations, and lives.

Rumors and gossip are the garbage of human communication. Bad talk taints the talker. Teach your children to leave gossip to the tabloids.

**I will show my children
that cheap shots can cost dearly.**

"Life is one long process of getting tired."
                                                          Samuel Butler

*M*others should never apologize for being tired. They earn their fatigue the old-fashioned way. They work for it!

Motherhood is exhausting. It's a tough job, but someone has to do it. Aren't you glad you were selected?

**I won't mind being bone-tired at the end
of the day. Lots of women would like
to trade places with me.**

"The law of heredity is that all undesirable traits come from the other parent."

Anon.

When there's trouble with the kids, too many mothers and fathers immediately resort to blaming each other. It doesn't help.

Finger-pointing and fault-finding don't solve problems. Working together may. It really doesn't matter who's to blame. It matters more who's going to do something about it.

Successful mothers look for answers, not excuses.

**I will work with my spouse to solve
our problems. We won't waste time
figuring out who's to blame.**

"Memory is the thing you forget with."
Alexander Chase

*M*emory distorts the past. It magnifies pleasant experiences and events while glossing over unhappy details. Many memories are altered images of a life we never lived.

Don't compare your child's experiences and accomplishments with what you recall of your own. It's unfair to measure today's reality against yesterday's fantasy. Don't haunt your child's life with ghosts from your own self-edited past.

**I will realize that I wasn't the perfect child
with the perfect childhood no matter
what I recall. The snow wasn't as deep
as I remember it either.**

*"The thing that impresses me most about America is
the way parents obey their children."*

Duke of Windsor, 1967

Some mothers allow their kids to take over and run the
family. It's not supposed to be that way. Children aren't
supposed to rule. Parents aren't supposed to be lackeys.

Be the parent. Make the rules and enforce them. Your
children will feel more secure as a result.

**I will make the rules.
I'm bigger, and it's my house.**

*"A picture has been said to be something between a
thing and a thought."*

Samuel Palmer

Every picture a child makes is a minimasterpiece. Children's drawings are the most honest art in the world. They give us a glimpse of how things look through a child's eyes.

Treasure what your child draws and keep it. You can't buy any other picture that will mean more to you.

**I will praise and keep whatever
my child draws. We will enjoy it together
in years to come.**

"What comes from the heart goes to the heart."
                              Samuel Taylor Coleridge

If you can't be anything else, you can be sincere in dealing with your children. Honest feelings provoke honest responses.

Your children will meet lots of phonies in this world. Don't be one of them. Show your children that sincerity is a sign of a well-adjusted person.

**I will be open and honest with my children.
What they see is what they get.**

"If anything is sacred, the human body is sacred."
Walt Whitman

 ome mothers spend so much time and energy caring for their children that they neglect themselves. That's not being unselfish. It's being foolish. Remember, your body is sacred too.

Do you want some sick woman raising your child? Pay attention to your own health. Take care of yourself. Healthy mothers have happier children.

**I will take care of myself
so I can take better care of my children.**

"There is no fear on our agenda."

Lyndon Johnson

easonable fear saves lives. Unreasonable fear ruins them.

Some people are so full of fear that there is no room for anything else. They miss out on the adventure of real living because they are afraid to take risks. They exist by cowering in the corner at the edge of life.

Help your child be unafraid to live. It's OK to fear danger. It's not OK to fear living. A full life requires courage and taking chances.

**I will keep fear out of my
child's life as much as possible.**

"Do unto your children as you would want them to do unto their children."

Ashleigh Brilliant

 he way you raise your children doesn't end there. Your children will tend to treat their offspring the same way you treat them.

Mothers are not only raising children; they're teaching how to raise children at the same time.

Makes you want to do it right, doesn't it?

———————— ————————

**I will try to be the best mother I can be.
I may be starting a trend.**

"Nothing is normally the hardest thing to do—but often it is the best."

Linus Mundy

It's possible for children to have too much mother. At some point kids need to try their wings, make mistakes, and figure things out on their own, without a mother's intervention or interference.

Sometimes the best thing a mother can do is nothing.

I will grit my teeth and do nothing if that's what it takes to help my child grow.

"Let your children grow tall and some taller than others if they have it in them to do so."

Margaret Thatcher

We never know a child's full potential. Don't put limits on your children's expectations or shrink their horizons with your own doubts. The best mothers don't furnish blinders or hobbles.

Let your children go and grow as far as they can. If something is going to get in their way, it won't be you.

I will urge my children to go as far as they can go, even if they're all going in different directions.

"We must develop and maintain the capacity to forgive."

Martin Luther King, Jr.

We need forgiveness in our world. Forgiveness is the lubricant that permits the engine of society to keep on running without backfiring.

People who don't forgive are stuck emotionally. They can't get beyond their bad feelings. Forgiveness feels good and lets you get on with your life.

Mothers are good at forgiveness. They practice it a lot. Pass on the skill of forgiving to your children.

I will teach my children that only petty people hold grudges. Healthy people let go, forgive, and move on.

"Why does God have a swear word for a name?"
                                        Samuel Montgomery

ids have lots of questions about God and religion. Guess who's supposed to have the answers?

Share what you know and believe about religion with your children. Don't assume they aren't interested.

**I will take my children to my house
of worship and explain what's
going on and why.**

"We live in an atmosphere of shame."
George Bernard Shaw

*S*hame can come from the inside. It should never come from the outside.

Blaming and shaming children are no better than battering and bullying them. Permanent harm can result from all of these.

Sensitive mothers don't heap shame on little children.

———————— ————————

**I will punish my children when needed,
but I will never shame them.**

"I must be cruel only to be kind."

William Shakespeare

Sometimes raising children means being hard-nosed, sticking to standards despite protest, and taking unpopular actions. Doing what children see as unfair and unreasonable is often in their best interest.

It's called "tough love." It takes someone tough to stick to it. Thank goodness for strong mothers!

**I will do what's right for my children
even if it hurts all of us for a little while.**

"Happy families are all alike; every unhappy family is unhappy in its own way."

Leo Tolstoy

*S*uccessful families all follow the simple, time-honored formula of honesty, mutual respect, compromise, and unconditional love. Unhappy families follow disparate routes to dysfunction.

There are all kinds of ways to mess up your family and your life. Wise mothers don't choose any of them.

I will learn from other successful parents (including my own) and will raise my child according to proven practices.

"Opera is where a guy gets stabbed in the back and instead of bleeding, he sings."

Ed Gardner

*S*ome people like rap. Some like rock. Some like rhythm and blues. Well-rounded men and women enjoy them all.

Expose your children to all kinds of music. It will expand their appreciation and enrich their lives. It wouldn't even hurt if you took them to an opera sometime.

**I will listen to different kinds
of music with my child.**

"Always do one thing less than you think you can do."

Bernard Baruch

$\mathcal{M}$otherhood makes for a fast-paced, hectic life. Some mothers keep pushing and going until they can't go anymore.

Be one of the smart ones. Stop before you drop. A rested mother is a better mother.

I will stop short of exhaustion. Doing too much isn't sacrifice; it's sabotage.

"If there's no dancing, count me out."

Emma Goldman

ance is acting out music. It's art, exercise, and fun all rolled together.

All children love to dance. They pick it up quickly and aren't afraid to fake it if they don't know the steps.

Too many adults, however, become self-conscious and stifle their love of dance. It's a sad loss.

Introduce your children to dance and encourage them to keep at it throughout life. It's hard to be down and dancing at the same time.

I will dance with my children.

"A child miseducated is a child lost."

John F. Kennedy

good education is still the best insurance policy for your children. There are lots of good schools out there. Find one and stick with it.

Greater learning usually means greater earning. Better yet, it means a richer life.

**I will do whatever it takes
to get a good education for my children.**

"Time is a circus always packing up and moving away."

Ben Hecht

ime waits not. Time wastes not. It's easy to spend time foolishly. Try not to do it.

Squeeze every moment. Get the most out of it you can. You won't get it back again.

**I will make wise use of my time.
The minutes of childhood aren't that many.**

"He who comes first eats first."

                            Eike von Repkow

The first shopper gets the bargains. The first moviegoer gets the good seats. The prize goes to the first person who crosses the finish line. There's always an edge in being first on the scene. Most people don't know this because they've never been there.

Teach your children the benefit of being a step ahead of the pack. It doesn't cost any more to be first in line.

**I will show my child the
advantage of being prompt—even early.**

"It takes a heap o' livin' in a house to make it home."

Edgar Guest

You can't make a family or a home overnight. A family is more than people living under the same roof. A home is more than four walls.

Lots of things have to happen before parents and children are a family and a house becomes a home. It takes working and surviving and laughing together. It takes good times and bad. It takes shared memories.

Stay the course. Build a history with your children. That's what makes a family and turns a house into a home.

——————— ———————

**I will be patient and willing to pay my dues
to build a lasting family.**

"Marriages are made in heaven—so are thunder and lightning."

Clint Eastwood

Don't expect "happily ever after." Nobody's family is perfect. The world's not that boring. Every family has problems. It's called life.

Expect lots of tests. That's how you know you've passed as a mother.

I will accept trouble but not defeat.

"There comes a time in a man's life when to get where he has to go—if there are no doors or windows—he walks through a wall."

Bernard Malamud

Do what you have to do to help your children succeed. If there are obstacles, go over, under, around, or through them.

Don't take no if yes is the only acceptable answer. Mothers have moved mountains. You can too if you have to.

—————— ——————

**I will go through a wall
for my child if necessary.**

"Two of life's futile words are 'If only—'."
                                                      Marjorie Holmes

*R*egrets and second-guessing won't raise your children.
Making decisions will.

Make the best choices you can and move on. Don't agonize and don't look back. If you make a bad decision, don't fret. You'll get a chance to make another one soon.

———————— ————————

**I will do what I think is best and leave
the *what ifs* and *if onlys* to others.**

"Every calling is great when it's greatly pursued."

Anon.

It's not what your children do when they grow up; it's how they do it. There can be glory in any walk of life.

It's a mother's job to prepare her children for life, not to plan their lives. They'll take care of that themselves. If you teach them that 100 percent is the only acceptable effort, you will have done enough.

**I will teach my children
to give their best every time.**

"Dare to be naive."

R. Buckminster Fuller

*S*ome people are so naive they still believe in old-fashioned values. They are honest, trusting, and hopeful. They tell the truth and keep their word and trust that others will do the same. Most mothers are in this group.

Naive people aren't stupid. They just choose to believe in themselves, in others, in life, and in the future. Naive people live in a nicer world than cynics do.

Let your children be naive for as long as they can.

I won't tell my children that the world isn't as pure as they think it is. If enough people believe it, it may come true.

"Dreams are necessary to life."

Anaïs Nin

𝒥f your child is a dreamer, don't knock it. Most miracles were someone's dreams first.

We need more dreams in this world. Reality isn't doing all that great.

**I will pray that my children's
dreams come true.**

"Fun is in very short supply."

Mike Veeck

$\mathcal{F}$amilies are funny things. Mom and Pop never went to parents' school, so they're inventing how to raise children as they go. The kids have never been kids before, so they don't know what they're supposed to do. Somehow, it all comes together.

Being a mother is a little like running an unrehearsed circus. The only sensible thing to do is enjoy it.

If you don't do anything else, have fun with your family. That's what you will all remember later on.

**I'll make sure none of us takes
life too seriously.**

"Insanity is hereditary; you can get it from your children."

Susan Levenson

*Y*our kids can drive you crazy if you let them. Don't let them.

The trick is to remember that they're the kids and you're the adult. If you act grown up, they'll grow up too. Sanity is contagious.

**I will keep my sanity while
those around me act a little crazy.**

241

"What this country needs are a few labor-making inventions."

Arnold Glason

*P*arents can make things too easy for their children. Life shouldn't be a free ride—even for kids. Children feel better about themselves, and parents do too, if kids work for some of what they get.

A child's life shouldn't be all work, but it should be some work. There's no other way to grow up.

I will let my children do some of the work.

"The loss of wonder is a condition leading to death of the soul."

Edmund Fuller

Childhood is a time of wonderment. To kids the world is full of magic and miracles. They aren't too sophisticated to be awestruck.

We can learn this from our children. Share your child's wonder. Take time to applaud a sunset together.

**I will permit myself to be in awe of the
world's wonders along with my children.**

"What is true anywhere is true everywhere . . .
all peoples cry, laugh, eat, worry and die."

Maya Angelou

Bigots aren't born. They're taught. Little children don't come with prejudice. They accept everyone equally. It's our job to keep them that way.

All mothers love their children. All children are worthy of love. These are the lessons mothers should teach.

**I will teach my children that all people
are more alike than different.**

"It's easier to do a job right than to explain why you didn't."

Martin Van Buren

Kids are good at slacking off, cutting corners, and making excuses. They do it because their agenda is different from an adult's.

You can (1) hassle your kids to do a sloppy job over and over until it's OK or (2) teach them to do the job right the first time and get it out of the way. Smart mothers choose number 2.

**I will teach my children
to do the right job right right away.**

"Education is teaching children to take pleasure in the right things."

Aristotle

Kids today are tempted by many pleasures. Not all of them are safe, socially acceptable, or legal. Just because it feels good doesn't mean it is good.

Children don't always know the difference. Mothers do. Don't be afraid to teach your children what's right and what's wrong. If you don't, who will?

**I will educate my children
about good fun and bad fun.**

"Love doesn't give failing grades."

Anon.

𝒩o child can fail in his mother's eyes. Mothers don't grade their children. Mothers just keep loving their children until they succeed.

**I will let my children know that there
are no tests in our family. Everybody passes!**

"Children are unpredictable. You never know what inconsistencies they're going to catch you in next."

Franklin P. Jones

ids need stability. Inconsistency and mixed messages mess them up.

Try to be steadfast with your children. They need to know that they can *always* count on you.

I will make sure my children don't have to worry about which mother is going to show up today.

"Hope is a risk that must be run."

George Barnanas

     hildren with no hope die before their time. Without hope, there is no place to go. Hope keeps us at it until we're done.

Give your children hope, because they are our only hope.

**I will have hope
so that my children may hope also.**

"I think parents should forget the genius bit—
what you want is a human being."

Jerome Bruner

ll mothers want to think their children are whiz kids. Mothers watch for signs of genius, brag whenever they can, press for high grades, and hope for college scholarships.

Most kids don't quite make it. There are very few geniuses in this world.

If your children turn out to be decent human beings, be satisfied and be proud. Smart is nice, but the human touch is more important.

I want my children to become responsible
adults. If they turn out to be bright
at the same time, that's OK too.

"Babies are such a nice way to start people."
                                        Don Herold

God knows what She is doing in starting people out as babies. It makes loving them natural and irresistible. If people started out as teenagers, there might be a lot fewer of them.

The bond a mother forges with her baby lasts a lifetime—even through the teenage years.

**I will remember that my gangling child
was once an innocent tiny baby and is
still the same person.**

"Any beast can cry over the misfortune of its own child. It takes a mensch to weep for others' children."
Sam Levenson

*M*others are mensches. Each mother's heart is large enough to hold the world's children.

All mothers love all children as their own. The club of motherhood is worldwide, and membership is for life. It's not an organization to mess around with.

I will love and watch out for other mothers' children as I know they would watch out for mine.

"No matter where you hide your sex magazines,
your teenager will find them."

Bruce Lansky

*N*o matter how hard you try, you can't hide sex from
your kids. They're going to find out about it.

It's better if they hear it first at home. The street version
often leaves out some crucial points.

Sex is too important for mothers to keep quiet about. You
might feel awkward talking to your children about sex, but
you'll feel a lot worse if you don't.

**I will not be too embarrassed to
talk to my children about sex.**

"Guilt: the gift that keeps on giving."
                                    Erma Bombeck

*G*uilt is a beast that never sleeps. Once you let it in and allow it to feed, it will only grow bigger and stronger until it consumes your life.

It can also consume your child's life. Let guilt into your home, and your child will get the idea that that's the way to respond to self-doubt.

Don't give guilt the time of day.

**The only thing I will feel guilty about is
any time I waste feeling guilty.**

"God intended motherhood to be a relay race."
                                        Mary Pride

*T*he wisdom of motherhood is passed on from one generation to the next. No mother stands completely alone.

Every mother possesses the collective knowledge of legions of mothers before her. It doesn't make the job easy, but it makes it possible.

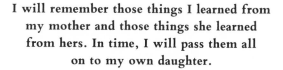

**I will remember those things I learned from
my mother and those things she learned
from hers. In time, I will pass them all
on to my own daughter.**

"Graffiti—memorable art too good to be published."
Edmund H. Volkart

*C*hildren can make art anywhere out of almost anything. They don't need a canvas or a fancy studio. The sidewalk or back fence will do.

Watch out for the impromptu artwork your child may produce in the most unlikely places. You don't want to miss out on a masterpiece.

I will put up a graffiti wall so my children can make art whenever they feel like it.

"God only knows and she ain't tellin'."

Paul Wilson

There are some things even mothers aren't meant to know. The full meanings and all the whys will never be understood.

It's OK. Mothers don't need to know everything. They know that things will work out, and that's all they need to know.

Being a mother is one part knowledge and nine parts faith!

———————— ————————

**I will live with things I cannot know
and have faith that we will make it.**

"We first make our habits, and then our habits make us."

John Dryden

From nail biting to knuckle cracking, kids pick up bad habits quickly and easily. These distracting behaviors just seem to move in and take up housekeeping almost overnight.

Do your children a favor by helping them weed out bad habits before they take root.

I will help my children stop bad habits before they start. In return, maybe they will help me correct some bad habits of my own.

"The most important factors in the life of their children are not the school, the television set, the playmates, or the neighborhood, but what the parents cherish, what they hate and what they fear."

Thomas Horg

W ho you are and what you believe go a long way in defining who your children will become. Be sure you are proud of who you are and what you stand for so you can be proud of what they will become.

A mother shapes her children most by expressing what she values.

I will take time to convey my values to my children.

"When the learner is ready, the teacher will appear."
Anon.

*Y*ou won't know all about child development when you start out as a mother. Not to worry. Most of what it takes to raise a child is learned on the job and as you go. When the time comes, you'll learn what to do. There is always a teacher available.

Motherhood is one of those journeys taken one step at a time.

I will do what I know today.
I will learn tomorrow's lessons tomorrow.

"Have you ever considered what the mere ability to read means? That it is the key which admits us to the whole world of thought and fancy and imagination."

James Russell Lowell

If the early bird gets the worm, it's probably because she was up early reading about worms and how to catch them.

Reading is an essential survival skill in our world. It lets us into the hearts and minds of the world's smartest people, past and present.

**I'll make sure my children know
they don't have to be happy to read
but have to read to be happy.**

"When the drug trip or alcohol binge is over, the problems will have remained the same or gotten worse."

A recovering sixteen-year-old

We live in an escapist society. Americans don't like problems. We want to hide, run away, find easy answers, or get quick fixes. That's why drugs are popular.

Drugs make things worse, not better. When you wake up, you still have the same problems—only now you have a hangover too.

I will teach my children that problems have to be solved. That's why we call them problems.

"The old law 'an eye for an eye' leaves everyone blind."

Martin Luther King, Jr.

Kids often want to get back at anyone who mistreats them. It's a natural response—for kids. Adults should know better.

Revenge isn't sweet. It doesn't work for nations, and it doesn't work for kids.

Retaliation just begets more retaliation. It becomes a contest to see who can sink the lowest. You don't want your child to end up at the bottom of the heap.

I will help my children find ways to solve disputes without getting back at people.

"Love is, above all, the gift of oneself."

Jean Anouilh

*L*ack of love is a child's greatest fear. Conversely, a child confident in a mother's love has no reason to fear anything.

Help keep your children safe from fear. Love them and let them know it.

---- ----

I will give my children the shield of my love.

"A hungry man knows no reason."
Hubert H. Humphrey

*D*on't expect to reason with your children, to hold a serious discussion, or to teach any great lessons when your children are hungry, tired, cold, or all of the above. Little children can't think beyond their physical needs. Their priorities are simple and straightforward.

Care for your children's physical needs before you try to address any deeper issues.

I will see to it that my children are fed and warm and rested. Then we will talk.

Things are in the saddle,
And ride mankind.

Ralph Waldo Emerson

*S*ome kids get too much stuff. They have so much they can't appreciate any of it. The more they have, the more they want. The having and the getting become a way of life.

The problem with making things the centerpiece of your existence is that all you end up with are things.

Don't make a big deal about things in your family. Make a big deal about people instead.

**I will teach my children that we should use
things and love people, not vice versa.**

"A letter is a gift to both the sender and the receiver."

Anon.

Letter writing is becoming a lost art. Everyone loves to get personal letters, but no one wants to write them. Telephone calls and fax messages are quick and easy. Letters require more effort and personal investment. That's what makes them special. E-mail is just technology. A letter is friendship in your own handwriting.

Teach your children to write personal letters, and you give them a unique link to the world.

I will help my child find a pen pal.

"Winter tames man, woman and beast."
                    William Shakespeare

Kids understand winter better than adults. Grown-ups think it's a time to hunker down and hide away inside. Children know that winter is a magical time for sliding, sledding, ice games, and snow fun. Compared to winter, other seasons are boring.

Don't sit out another winter. Join your child in outdoor winter activities. You may be surprised by how warm it feels to play together in the cold.

───────────   ───────────

**I will help my children build a snow fort.
Then I will make some hot chocolate
for all of us.**

"This very love must help the child grow away from the mother and become fully independent."

Erich Fromm

*R*aising children is a lot about growing up and going away. Most mothers are good at starting out as parents but have difficulty finishing the job. The going-away part is hard.

Be prepared for the good-byes and be ready to say them gracefully. That's what you've worked toward all those years.

Instead of grieving over my diminished role, I will celebrate my child's growing independence.

"There are two ways to look at things. One is that nothing is a miracle. The other is that everything is."
Albert Einstein

$\mathcal{M}$others don't make good cynics or skeptics, because mothers believe in miracles and happy endings. They have to. They work with them every day.

Never cease to be astonished by the miracles that your children are.

**I will refuse to become cynical.
It's hard not to believe in angels
once you've had little babies.**

"If you seek my monument, look around you."
Sir Christopher Wren

If there were a Mother's Hall of Fame, all mothers would be inducted into it. Actually, you don't need a Hall of Fame.

Your children are your monument and their lives are your legacy. Who could want more?

I will know that what I am doing will last.

"There is no security in this life, only opportunity."
Douglas MacArthur

*N*othing is certain in this world. Mothers can't give their children guarantees. The best you can do is give your kids as many chances and choices as possible.

You can't lock in success for your children, but you can be sure they're not locked out of possibilities.

**I will open as many doors as possible
for my children and let them choose
which ones to go through.**

ABOUT THE AUTHOR

Dr. Robert D. Ramsey is a lifelong educator and free-lance writer from Minneapolis. During his thirty-five-year career as teacher, counselor, and educational leader, he has worked with mothers and children from all kinds of families.

Throughout his distinguished career, Dr. Ramsey's writings have been popular with parents and professionals alike. His most recent publications include *Administrator's Complete School Discipline Guide* (Prentice-Hall) and *501 Ways to Boost Your Child's Self-Esteem* (Contemporary Books).

As a child raised by a single parent, a parent and grandparent himself, and a professional educator and author, Dr. Ramsey knows what it takes to raise kids today. His books have helped countless parents and educators do a better job. *Mother's Wisdom* can now do the same for mothers everywhere.